GREAT AMERICAN QUILTS 1990

GREAT AMERICAN QUILTS 1990

Compiled and Edited by

Sandra L. O'Brien

©1989 by Oxmoor House, Inc.
Book Division of Southern Progress Corporation
P.O. Box 832463, Birmingham, AL 35201

Library of Congress Catalog Number: 86-62283
ISBN: 0-8487-0799-0
ISSN: 0890-8222
Manufactured in the United States of America
First Printing 1989

Executive Editor: Nancy J. Fitzpatrick
Production Manager: Jerry Higdon
Associate Production Manager: Rick Litton
Art Director: Bob Nance

Great American Quilts 1990

Editor: Sandra L. O'Brien
Editorial Assistant: Alice L. Cox
Copy Chief: Mary Jean Haddin
Designer: Melinda P. Goode
Patterns and Illustrations: Larry Hunter, Rick Tucker, Chuck Farmer
Production Assistant: Theresa L. Beste
Photographers: Colleen Duffley, Gary Clark, Mary-Gray Hunter, Howard L. Puckett, Kim Appel, Jim Bathie

To find out how you can order *Cooking Light* magazine, write to *Cooking Light*®, P.O. Box C-549, Birmingham, AL 35283.

CONTENTS

EDITOR'S NOTE 6
Preliminary Instructions 6
Quilt Documentation 6
Triangular Template Placement for Piecing
    Stars from Striped Fabric 6
Backing 7

STARMAKERS 8
Charlotte Cameron 10
Summer Stars

Margaret Y. Yates 13
Triple Spin

Dixie Haywood 16
Hoshi Sensu

Lorraine Salamone 22
Heart's Desire

The Elliotts, the Sewards, the Joyces,
    the Pinkuses, and Martha Babcock 26
Thanksgiving Star

Elaine De Lancey Shinners 30
Folded-Stars Bridal Quilt

Elizabeth J. Contessa Wuts 34
Star-Spangled Banner Scrap Variation

Linda Goodmon Emery 39
Some Are the Same

Christine Schnaufer 44
Judy's Star Surrounded

Donna Lake 48
Starry Castle

Pauline Spieks 54
Star and Crescent

Susan Craig Campbell 58
Starflower

QUILTS ACROSS AMERICA......62

Carol Doak...............................64
Comical Country

Michaeline Reed..........................71
Compass Quest I

Pauline Spieks...........................76
Williamsburg Palm

Susan Denise Brucker.....................82
Basket Full of Memories

Ann M. Hargis...........................88
Migration

Donna Lake..............................92
Ribbons 'n Rings

Hope Shoaf..............................96
Hope's Double Nine Patch

Tommi Marten............................99
Tommi's Castle Wall

Patricia Eaton..........................102
Bear's Paw

TRADITIONS IN QUILTING....106

Barbara Ellen Middy Russell &
   Helen Louise Lindsey.................108
Whig Rose, Cherry

Elizabeth R. Lawrence...................114
Cathedral Window

Angeline Lewis Pond &
   Hattie Pond Fleming.......116
Prairie Star, Rail Fence II

BEE QUILTERS.................122

Kentucky Heritage Quilt Society...........124
Ryder's Star

Midland Quilters Guild...................128
Ohio Star with Houses

Quilt San Diego........................132
1,001 Nights

DESIGNER GALLERY...........138

Dixie Haywood..........................140
Fruit of the Bloom

Susan Webb Lee.........................141
Thunder and Lightning

Michaeline Reed........................142
Flights of Fancy

Linda Goodmon Emery....................143
Persian Paisley

RESOURCES.....................144

EDITOR'S NOTE

Longfellow called the stars the forget-me-nots of the angels, and many quilted stars, made by a host of quilting angels, have come to reside in the pages of *Great American Quilts 1990*.

"Starmakers," our special chapter for 1990, features 12 out-of-this-world star quilts. There are summer stars, starflowers, and starry castles, to name a few, just waiting to light up your home. For special effects, their starlight merges with the brightness of still more stars, which grace the pages of our other quiltmaking chapters—"Quilts Across America," "Traditions in Quilting," and "Bee Quilters." These chapters are teeming with fields of starry quilts to make. But if your neck aches from too much stargazing, there are plenty of quilts, such as *Williamsburg Palm*, *Migration*, *Comical Country*, and *Cherry*, to bring your focus back to earth. And take a side trip through our museum of quilted one-of-a-kinds in "Designer Gallery" and receive an outpouring of inspiration.

Sprinkled among our quilting angels and quilted stars are tidbits of information about quilt documentation and triangular template placement on striped fabrics. We've peeked at the backs of our quilts to emphasize the importance of quilt documentation. Review the paragraph below and then take a glimpse at the inscriptions made by the quiltmakers in this book.

Besides these, we have our must-read Preliminary Instructions and a feature on backing, that often neglected and unsung hero of quiltmaking.

Preliminary Instructions

All pattern pieces include ¼" seam allowance. All measurements for pieces, sashing, and border strips are given *including* seam allowances, unless otherwise noted. Some oversize pieces are placed on a grid.

Fabric requirements are based on 44"/45"-wide fabric with trimmed selvages, and requirements for backing on bed quilts are based on a three-panel backing. *Generous allowances are given for fabric requirements to account for fabric shrinkage and individual differences in cutting.* Fabric requirements are given for one-piece borders. We suggest that you wash, dry, and press fabrics before using. Finished quilt size is the size of the quilt before quilting.

Quilt Documentation

Never take it for granted that your husband, children, siblings, or friends will remember when, for what purpose, or for whom you made a quilt. Documentation is especially important if a quilt is to be sold or given as a gift. Information should include the name of the quilt, the quiltmaker, city and state, date, and quilt pattern. Special thoughts or feelings about the quilt and any other particulars, such as an unusual incident that happened while making the quilt, names of friends who assisted you, or kinds of fabrics used, can be included.

As you thumb through these pages, you will find photographs of the different ways our quilters chose to document their quilts. The most prevalent methods are messages typed on muslin, using a manual typewriter, or a handwritten note with a permanent marking pen. The muslin is appliquéd to the quilt's back and, as you will see, embellished in numerous ways.

Triangular Template Placement for Piecing Stars from Striped Fabrics

Many of our star quilts use triangles to make their stars. When using a striped fabric, it is especially helpful to use the two-mirror method of looking at the fabric before cutting. (See sketch.) This saves fabric and time, while also stimulating

a fresh way of looking at the design possi-
bilities. Move the mirrors across the fabric to
find the ideal placement for the template. To aid
in fabric cutting, make your templates from a
clear plastic material and mark part of the fabric
design on the template.

Backing

Are you a quilt-top snob?—too busy with the
top to be concerned about what's on the
back of a quilt. For us quilt top snobs,
a glance at the back to look at the
stitching satisfies our curiosity; then we
return to surveying the top. Some of us
have such an affinity for the quilt top that
once it is completed, the backing becomes an
afterthought. We spend hours and hours carefully
cutting and piecing a beautiful top. Then, because
we are anxious to move on to the quilting, we
often hastily seam fabric sections together, giving
little thought or care to the backing.

More and more, the flip side of the quilt is
being recognized, because it is often as interesting
and intriguing as the front. Quilters are using
print and floral fabrics for backing, as well as cle-
verly inserting a few patchwork patterns. Mind
you, quilt backs will never replace the importance
of the quilt top, but the next time you examine a
bed quilt, try starting via "the rear window of
quilting" for a different perspective. The back
will say a lot about the quilter. And best of all,
you will find that there's a lot going on! Below
are some hints to remember about the backing
for a bed quilt.

1. The type of fabric used for the backing should
be compatible with, or identical to, the fabric
used in the top.

2. Percale sheets are not recommended for backing, because they are so tightly woven that they
make hand quilting difficult.

3. The backing fabric should be a color that is
compatible with the fabrics used in the top so
that there is no shadowing through to the front.
Prints are acceptable, but, again, be sure that the
design does not shadow through to the front.

4. Bed quilts should have a three-panel backing
with vertical seams. The three-panel backing is
recommended because it tends to wear better and
lie flatter than the two panel, whose seam often
makes a ridge down the center of the quilt. Side

| |
| Center Panel |
| Side Panel   Side Panel |

Quilt Backing Diagram

panels should be equal in size. (See Quilt Backing
Diagram.)

5. Trim selvages of backing panels.

6. Use a ½″ seam allowance for joining backing
panels.

7. Backing seams should be pressed closed. Press-
ing the seams open weakens them.

8. Cut backing at least 2″ larger than the quilt
top on all four sides.

9. Trim excess backing fabric after quilting is
complete.

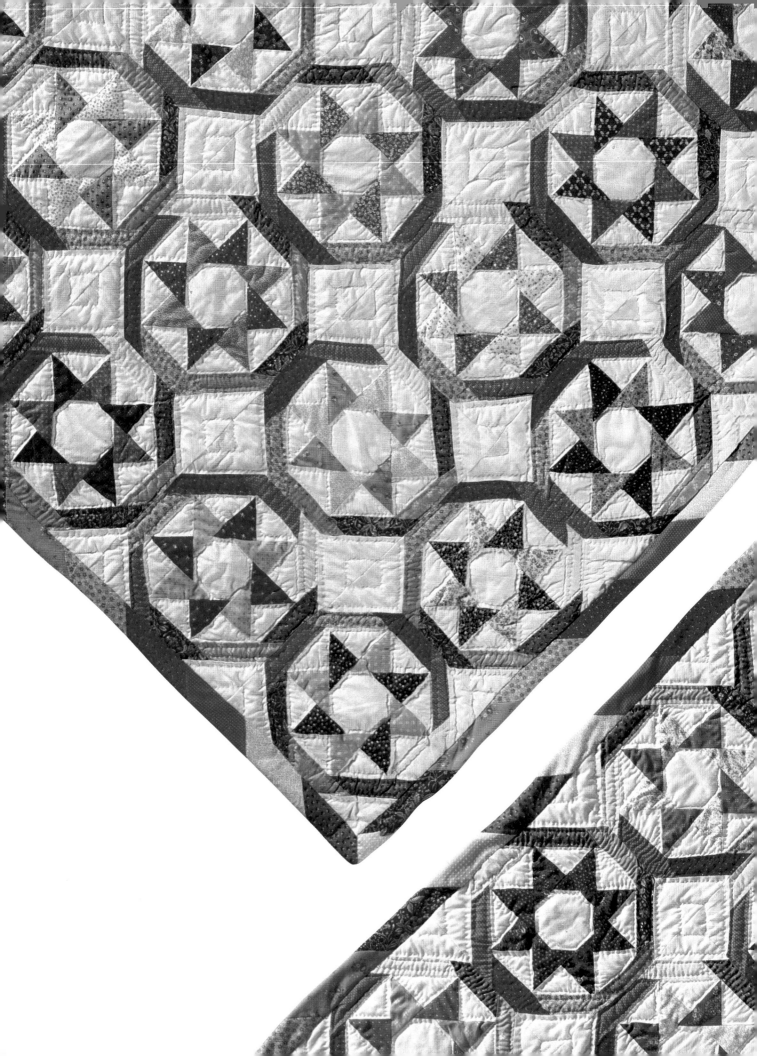

STARMAKERS

Charlotte Cameron

Glenshaw, Pennsylvania

"Quilting is a happy, sunny part of my life," says Charlotte. "I often go to sleep thinking of this or that pattern or fabric." Sewing and quilting have so enriched her life that she wishes everyone had an interest that offered so much pleasure.

Charlotte is a member of the North Pittsburgh Quilters Guild and finds quilting with friends especially gratifying.

Summer Stars
1988

This prismatic cascade of stars was Charlotte's first quilt. "Scrap quilts are my favorite," says Charlotte, "but I prefer the look of a planned scrap quilt—not just a hodgepodge of any fabric." Charlotte was inspired to empty her scrap basket and make a quilt, after looking at the Texas Star quilt pictured in Judy Martin's book, *Scrap Quilts*. (See "Resources.")

There are 185 different fabrics in Charlotte's *Summer Stars*, and every one of the 400 stars was pieced by hand. "This quilt will always be my favorite," says Charlotte. "I love looking at it and thinking—I did that!"

Summer Stars

Finished Quilt Size
Approximately 100″ x 110″

Number of Stars and Finished Size
400 stars—approximately 5″ x 5″

Fabric Requirements
Pastel scrap prints★

Blues	—1¾ yd. total
Pinks	—1¾ yd. total
Greens	—1¾ yd. total
Oranges	—1¾ yd. total
Yellows	—1¾ yd. total
White	—4¼ yd.
Backing	—9½ yd.

★Scrap yardage requirement for one star is 4″ x 8″.

Number to Cut

Diamond	—480 blues
	480 pinks
	480 greens
	480 oranges
	480 yellows
	1,121 white

Quilt Top Assembly
1. Join 6 diamonds of the same color group to form a star, as shown in Star Piecing Diagram. Make 400 stars.

Star Piecing Diagram

2. Alternate 20 stars of the same color group with 19 white diamonds and join, as shown in Star Row Piecing Diagram. Make 20 rows.
3. Arrange star rows in the following color order: blue, pink, green, orange, yellow. Repeat order 3 more times. (See quilt photograph.) Join rows with white diamonds, as shown in Setting Diagram.

Quilting
Outline-quilt ¼″ inside seam line of star edge to form a quilted star. Quilt ½″ from that line of quilting to repeat star pattern in center of each star. Outline-quilt ¼″ inside seam line of all white diamonds.

Finished Edges
Charlotte turned under the edges of her quilt top and the edges of her quilt back to face each other and blindstitched the edges together to form an unbound edge.

Quilt Documentation
Charlotte cross-stitched an original border design around her documentation in the colors that matched her quilt fabric. (See photograph of quilt documentation.) She included the number of pieces, inclusive dates, and a number one in the border to indicate that this was her first quilt.

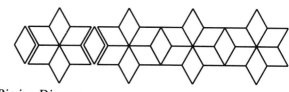

Star Row Piecing Diagram

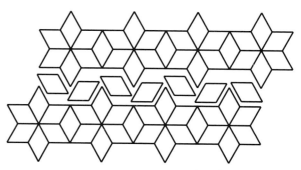

Setting Diagram

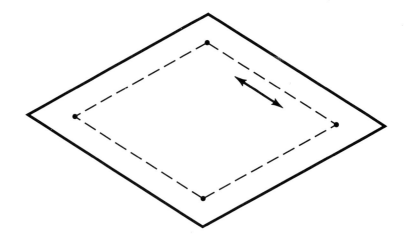

When you talk with Margaret, you instantly sense the strong love she has for her family. With no regrets, she sacrificed many hours of personal-interest time (and that included quilting) to meet the needs of bedridden loved ones. Now that much of that commitment is over, she has more time for herself, and her thoughts and focus in life have returned to quilting.

About 10 years ago, Margaret made her first quilt, a scrap quilt for her husband. Says Margaret, "I decided then that quilting was a way in which I could leave a memento for my family."

Margaret's quilts have each won several ribbons, and in 1987 her quilt, *Discussing the Constitution*, was selected as the representative for Kentucky in the "We the Quilters" competition that commemorated the bicentennial of the Constitution.

Margaret Y. Yates
Rural Retreat, Virginia

Triple Spin
1988

Triple Spin is a *pas de deux* of veteran quilt blocks, each anchored *en pointe* ("the first two spins"), embraced by arcs of quilting ("the third spin"). "So many people talk about the spinning effect of a quilt," says Margaret, "that I thought that I would like to try a real spinner." Performing this triple spin are Star of the West, also known as Harry's Star or Clay's Choice, and Cube Lattice. Margaret was inspired to combine traditional blocks by suggestions made in *The It's Okay If You Sit On My Quilt Book* by Mary Ellen Hopkins.

We found Margaret to be a tried-and-true starmaker, for in each square of the Cube Lattice block, a star is quilted. "I find myself using stars in everything," says Margaret.

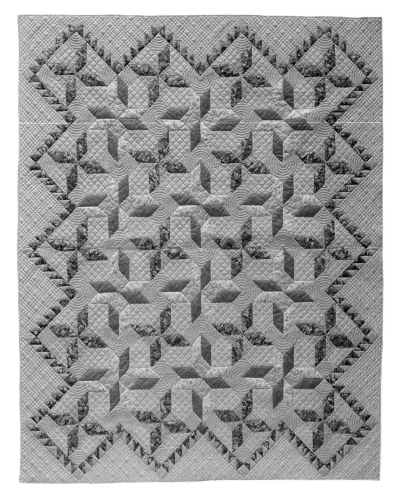

Fabric Combination	Number of Pieced Squares
Navy floral/navy print	80
Navy floral/blue print	80
Blue floral/purple print	48
Blue floral/blue print	48
Purple print/blue print	48

2. Join navy floral/navy print squares, navy floral/blue print squares, blue print squares (A), and lavender squares (A), as shown in Star of the West Piecing Diagram. Join in 4 rows of 4 squares each and join rows to complete block. Make 20 blocks.

3. Join remaining pieced squares and lavender squares (A), as shown in Cube Lattice Piecing Diagram. Join in 4 rows of 4 squares each and join rows to complete block. Make 12 blocks. (Arrow indicates top of block.)

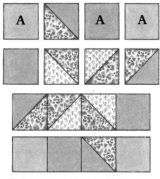

Star of the West Piecing Diagram

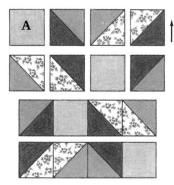

Cube Lattice Piecing Diagram

🟦 *blue print* 🟦 *blue floral* 🟦 *purple print*
⬜ *lavender* ⬜ *navy print* ⬜ *navy floral*

4. Using the quick pieced-squares method, make 164 pieced squares from navy floral and navy print fabrics. Mark a grid of 2⅞″ squares on top fabric. Each 18″ x 22″ rectangle should make 84 pieced squares.

Triple Spin

Finished Quilt Size
74″ x 92″

Number of Blocks and Finished Size
20 Star of the West
blocks—12″ x 12″
12 Cube Lattice blocks—12″ x 12″

Fabric Requirements
Navy floral	—2½ yd.
Navy print	—1¾ yd.
Blue print	—4 yd.
Blue floral	—1½ yd.
Purple print	—1 yd.
Lavender	—1¼ yd.
Blue print for bias binding	—1¼ yd.
Backing	—5½ yd.

Number to Cut
Template A	—80 blue print
	128 lavender
Template B	—14 navy floral
	18 navy print

Quilt Top Assembly
1. All of Margaret's pieced squares were made by using the quick machine-piecing method. Lay two fabric rectangles of equal size with right sides together. (We suggest a 18″ x 22″ rectangle.) For example, if you want to make a navy floral and navy print pieced square, then one rectangle should be navy floral and one navy print. Mark a grid of 3⅞″ squares on the top fabric, as shown in Pieced Squares Diagram. Draw a diagonal line through each square, as shown. Machine-stitch ¼″ on each side of diagonal lines. Cut along marked lines. This size rectangle should make 40 pieced squares. Refer to table below and make the number of pieced squares indicated.

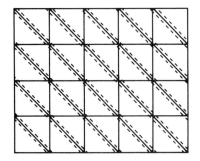

Pieced Squares Diagram

5. Make border strips from navy floral/navy print pieced squares, navy print squares (B), navy floral squares (B), as shown in Border Strip Diagram below and quilt photograph.

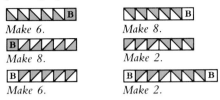

Make 6. Make 8.

Make 8. Make 2.

Make 6. Make 2.

Border Strip Diagram

■ *navy floral* □ *navy print*

6. Arrange Star of the West (SW) blocks and Cube Lattice (CL) blocks in diagonal rows, as shown in Setting Diagram I. (Arrows indicate top of block.) Join at sides to form rows and join a border strip to each end, as shown.

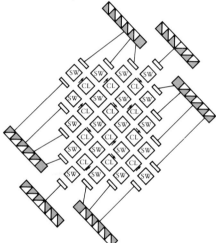

Setting Diagram I

7. Join border strips to the ends of rows, as shown in Setting Diagram II. Match seam lines and join rows.

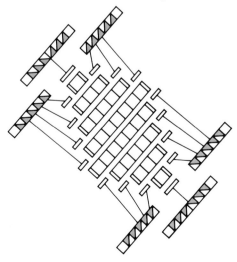

Setting Diagram II

8. Cut 4 corner right triangles, each with a 17″ hypotenuse (includes seam allowance), from blue print. Center and join to quilt, as shown in Setting Diagram III.

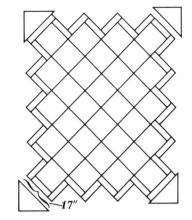

17″

Setting Diagram III

9. Cut 14 right triangles with 13″ sides (includes seam allowance) from blue print. Join triangles to quilt in order shown in Setting Diagram IV. Triangles will overlap each other at corners.

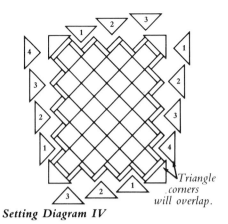

Triangle corners will overlap.

Setting Diagram IV

Quilting
A star was quilted in the center of each lavender square of the Cube Lattice blocks. Partial concentric circles, ½″ apart, were quilted in the remaining lavender squares. A 1″ cross-hatching pattern was quilted on the remainder of the blocks. Border triangles were quilted in a varied cross-hatching pattern. (See quilt photograph.)

Finished Edges
Bind with blue print fabric.

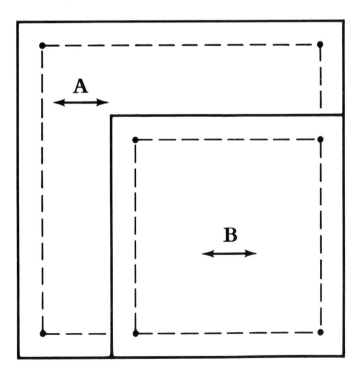

15

Dixie Haywood

Pensacola, Florida

Throughout her remarkable career as a quilt teacher, designer, award winner, and writer, Dixie tells us, the non-quilting rewards are the things that have enriched her life the most. "The chance to travel, the ability to help three children through college, the opportunity to help others learn the joy of quilting," says Dixie, "and the deep and lasting friendships with women of all ages, backgrounds, and experiences are just a few of them." But even if quilting itself were the only perk, Dixie tells us that she would continue to quilt. "Quilting, first and always, satisfies my need to work with fabric in a creative way," says Dixie. "I am a professional whose work is a pleasure!"

Dixie's quilts are frequently showstoppers and award winners. Her *Red Cubes* quilt won first place in the Masters Division, Art Quilt Category, at the 1987 American International Quilt Association Judged Show in Houston, Texas. Sometimes her quilts tell a story, as with *Fruit of the Bloom*. Turn to our "Designer Gallery" chapter and observe the fate of any watermelon found in Dixie's household.

Hoshi Sensu (Star Fan)
1987

The fans that grace Dixie's *Hoshi Sensu* are versions of motifs found in many traditional Japanese family crests. (See "Resources.") Dixie was drawn to make this quilt for two reasons: first, because her daughter-in-law's father is Japanese-American; and second, because she was able to use two familiar quilt motifs, the fan and the star. Dixie extended the Japanese theme to the borders by appliquéing another family crest design on them. A simple wood sorrel design is also found several times on each fan in a quilted format.

Hoshi Sensu won the Judges' Choice and First Place in Mixed Techniques ribbons at Pensacola Quilts!, 1987, Pensacola, Florida, and is featured in the *1989 American Quilt Calendar*.

Hoshi Sensu (Star Fan)

Finished Quilt Size
90″ x 112″

Number of Blocks and Finished Size
12 blocks—16½″ x 16½″

Fabric Requirements

Cream	—6 yd.
Med. green	—⅞ yd.
Dk. green	—3¼ yd.
Rust print	—6 yd.
Solid rust	—⅞ yd.
Tan	—⅞ yd.
Yellow	—⅞ yd.
Brown	—⅞ yd.
Dk. green for bias binding	—1¼ yd.
Backing	—9½ yd.

Other Materials
Freezer paper
Fabric-compatible glue stick

Number to Cut

Template A	—12 solid rust
	12 med. green
	12 tan
	12 yellow
	12 brown
Template B	—12 solid rust
	12 med. green
	12 tan
	12 yellow
	12 brown
Template C	—60 solid rust
	60 med. green
	60 tan
	60 yellow
	60 brown
Template D	—240 cream
Template E★	—12 solid rust
	12 med. green
	12 tan
	12 yellow
	12 brown
Template F	—48 dk. green
Template G	—130 rust print
Template H	—20 rust print
Template I	—10 rust print
Template J	—4 dk. green
Template K★	—42 rust print

★See steps 3 and 9 before cutting fabrics.

Quilt Top Assembly
1. Join pieces (A, B, C) of same color and piece (D), as shown in Fan Piecing Diagram. Make 12 fans of each color (solid rust, med. green, tan, yellow, and brown).

Fan Piecing Diagram

Block Assembly Diagram I

2. Cut twelve 17″ squares from cream. Center fans on cream blocks with one fan at center top and baste in place, as shown in Block Assembly Diagram I. On each successive block, rotate the color of the center fan clockwise. (See quilt photograph.) (Note: When spacing the fans equally from the edge of the background, the center of the fan *will not* be at the center of the background.) Appliqué fans to block.
3. Trace fan's tail pattern (E) *without* seam allowance on dull side of freezer paper. Cut out on traced

line. Make 60. Iron 12 on each fan color, shiny side down, on wrong side of fabric along lengthwise or crosswise grain of fabric. Cut fabric, leaving a ¼″ seam allowance. Turn seam allowance to back of paper and baste the seam allowance over the edge of the freezer paper. (Some quilters may prefer to stick down the seam allowance with fabric glue.) Appliqué tail to block, as shown in Block Assembly Diagram I. Cut out fabric from behind fan pieces and remove freezer paper.

18

4. Cut 4 strips, 1¼″ wide, from dk. green to frame each block. (Measurement includes seam allowance.) Join strips to block. Join piece (F) to corners, as shown in Block Assembly Diagram II. Trim excess fabric from corners. Repeat for remaining blocks.

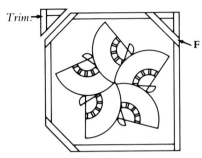

Block Assembly Diagram II

5. Cut 31 sashing strips, 4½ wide, from rust print. (See Row Assembly Diagram.)

Alternate 4 sashing strips with 3 blocks to form a row. Join at sides, *stitching up to seam lines* when joining. Make 4 rows.

6. Join pieces (G, H, I) to make partial and whole octagons, as shown in Sashing Assembly Diagram. Make 10 whole octagons and 10 partial octagons. (Octagons will be trimmed when borders are added.)

Alternate partial and whole octagons with sashing strips to form a sashing row, as shown in Sashing Assembly Diagram. Make 3 sashing rows. Make 2 more sashing rows, as shown in Sashing Assembly Diagram for Top and Bottom Rows.

7. Alternate sashing rows with block rows, beginning with the sashing row for the top, and join. Trim octagons even with sashing strips. *Square* corners.

8. Cut 4 borders, 2½″ wide, from dk. green and join to quilt. Join piece (J) to corners in same manner as piece (F) was joined to each block. Trim excess fabric from corners. (See quilt photograph.)

9. Cut 4 borders, 6½″ wide, from cream and join to quilt. Cut 4 strips, 6½″ wide, from cream. Join across corners and trim as before.

Space motifs (K) along cream border and appliqué in place. (You may choose to use the freezer paper method, explained in step 3, to appliqué these motifs in place.)

10. Cut 4 borders, 2½″ wide, from dk. green and join to quilt. Cut 4 strips, 2½″ wide, from dk. green. Join across corners and trim.

Quilting

Outline-quilt around all fans. Follow the curve of the fans with quilting lines, ¾″ apart. (See quilt photograph.) Quilt three wood sorrel motifs in each fan. Outline-quilt outside the dk. green framing strips of each block. A 1″ diamond grid is quilted on all sashing strips and extended to include the triangles (G) on each end of the strip. The remaining triangles (G) are accent-quilted by following the design of the print.

Outline-quilt around appliquéd motif (K) on cream borders. Quilt curve lines, 1″ apart, across all three borders. (See quilt photograph.)

Finished Edges

Bind with dk. green fabric.

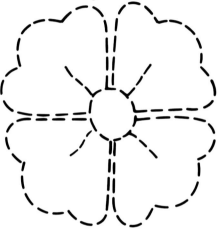

Wood Sorrel Quilting Pattern

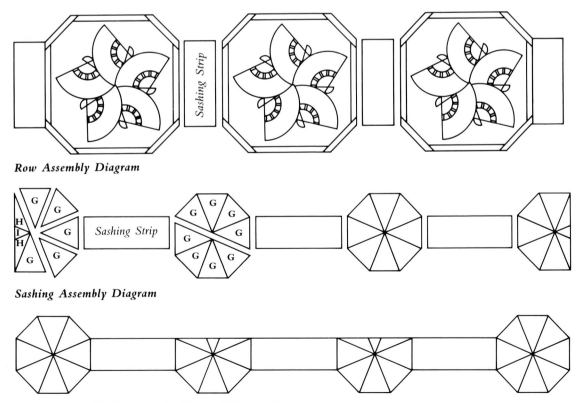

Row Assembly Diagram

Sashing Assembly Diagram

Sashing Assembly Diagram for Top and Bottom Rows

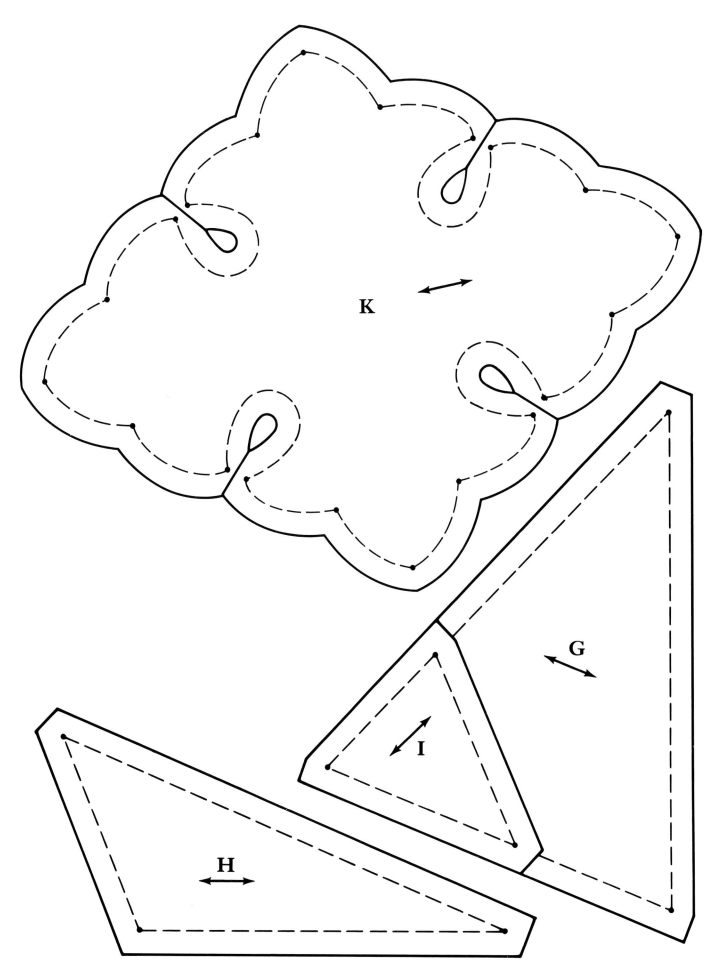

K

G

I

H

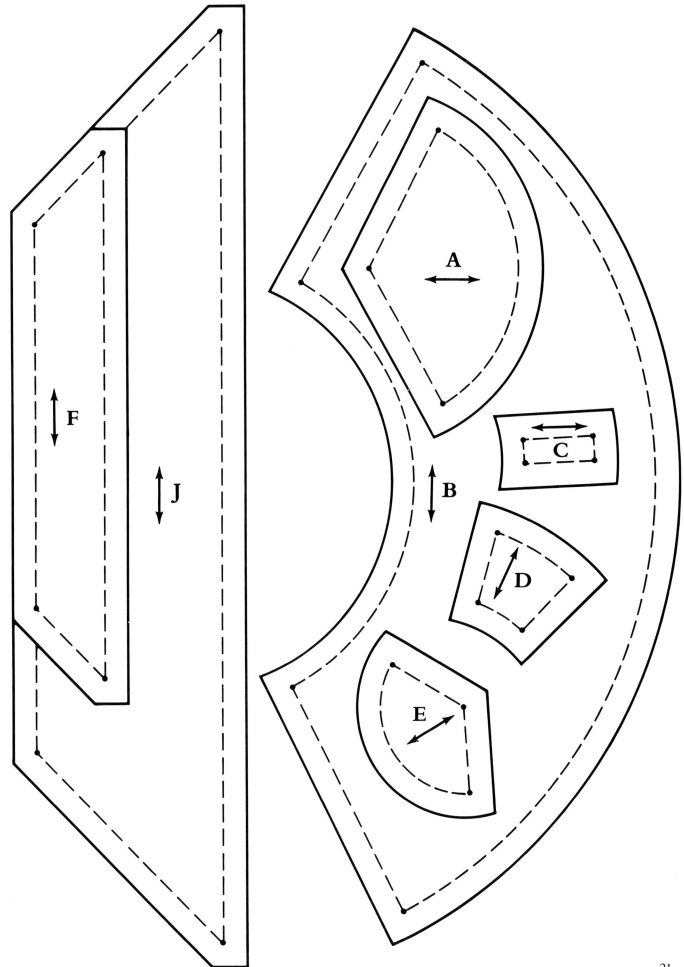

21

Heart's Desire
1986

"This is the quilt I am most proud of," says Lorraine. It was made for her daughter Diana, who selected the pattern, colors, and fabrics. The pattern resembles the traditional pattern, The Little Giant or Heart's Desire. Lorraine chose the latter name because during the time of its making, she watched the love between her daughter and future son-in-law, Michael, grow. "The quilt is as beautiful as the love that they share," says Lorraine.

"Quilts have longevity," says Lorraine. "Pictures are removed and replaced, clothes are outgrown, but a quilt goes on and on, whispering its message to those who have the privilege of owning it. Oh, how I wish I had started quilting sooner."

Having begun sewing at an early age, Lorraine admired the artistry of quiltmaking for many years before attempting it. "I have done crewel, needlepoint, and embroidery," says Lorraine, "but nothing has excited me as much as quilting."

Lorraine wants her quilts not only to be meaningful to her but also to the receiver. "I usually enclose a poem with each quilt," says Lorraine, "to tell them why I chose that pattern."

Lorraine Salamone

Bethpage, New York

Heart's Desire

Finished Quilt Size
84″ x 108″

Number of Blocks and Finished Size
12 blocks—16″ x 16″

Fabric Requirements
Black print — 4½ yd.
White print — 4¼ yd.
Blue with white
  pindots* — 3 yd.
Pink print — ½ yd.
Black print for
  bias binding — 1¼ yd.
Backing — 6½ yd.
*Throughout the directions, blue with white pindots will be designated as blue.

Number to Cut
Template A — 48 black print
  48 white print
Template B — 96 blue
Template C — 48 black print
Template D — 96 white print
Template E — 96 black print
Template E** — 96 black print
Template F — 96 white print
Template G — 48 white print
Template H — 20 pink print
**Flip or turn over template if fabric is one-sided.

Quilt Top Assembly
1. Alternate 4 black print pieces (A) with 4 white print pieces (A) and join, as shown in Block Piecing Diagram I. Join trapezoids (B) together and then join to block, as shown in Block Piecing Diagram II.

Join triangles (D) to sides of triangle (C), as shown in Block Piecing Diagram III. Join triangles (E) to triangle (F), as shown, twice. Join pieced rectangles at ends to form a strip, as shown, and join to block sides. Make strips for block top and bottom and join a square (G) to each end, as shown. Join to block. Make 12 blocks.

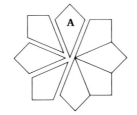

Block Piecing Diagram I

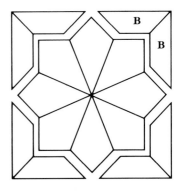

Block Piecing Diagram II

Block Piecing Diagram III

2. Cut 24 sashing strips, 2½″ x 16½″, from blue. Join to opposite sides of each block.
3. Cut 24 sashing strips, 2½″ x 20½″, from blue. Join to top and bottom of each block.
4. Cut 62 sashing strips, 2″ x 20½″, from white print. Cut 31 sashing

strips, 1½" x 20½", from black print. Set a black print strip between white print strips and join. Make 31 pieced-sashing strips.

5. Alternate 4 pieced-sashing strips with 3 blocks and join to form a row. Make 4 rows.

6. Alternate 4 squares (H) with 3 pieced-sashing strips and join to form a sashing row. Make 5 sashing rows.

7. Alternate sashing rows with block rows, beginning with a sashing row, and join.

8. Cut 2 borders, 4½" wide, from black print and join to sides of quilt. Cut 2 borders, 4½" wide, from black print and join to top and bottom of quilt.

Quilting
Quilt Heart's Desire blocks and sashing, as shown in Quilting Diagram. Lorraine's border is quilted in an unbroken rope pattern.

Finished Edges
Bind with black print fabric.

Quilting Diagram

Quilting Pattern

Heart Quilting Pattern

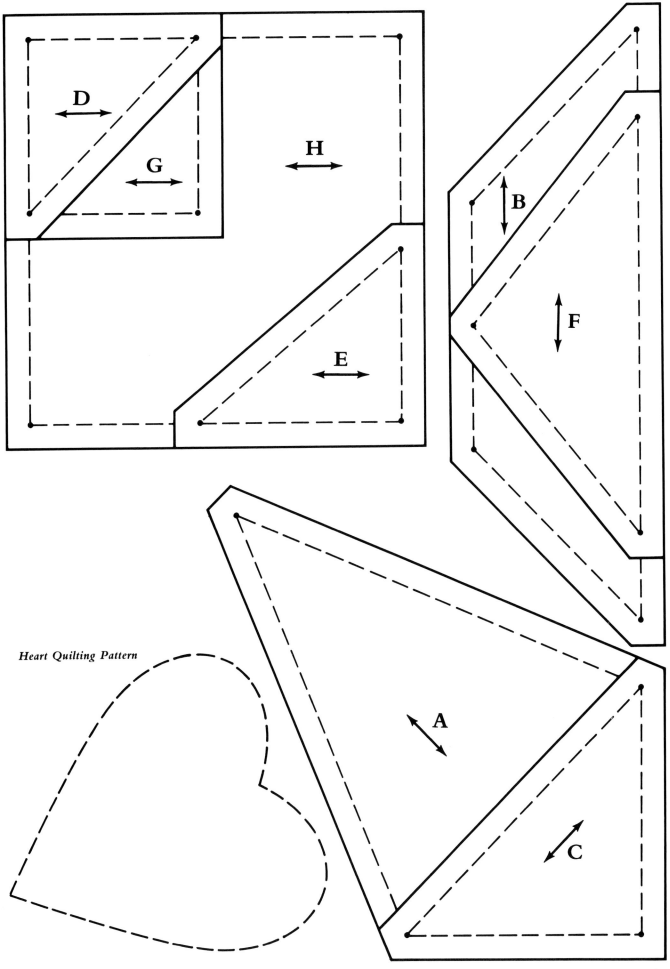

Heart Quilting Pattern

D

G

H

E

B

F

A

C

25

The Elliotts, the Sewards, the Joyces, the Pinkuses, & Martha Babcock

Butler, Pennsylvania

Susan Elliott

Let the stars shine on Thanksgiving! Sixteen stitchers, some novice, some expert, make Thanksgiving a star-studded event. They come from all over the United States, from California, Arizona, and Indiana, and meet at the home of Tom and Susan Elliott in Pennsylvania for a very special holiday tradition. It's a time to be thankful and enjoy a scrumptious Thanksgiving dinner, and it's a time to piece a star quilt!

Susan's sister, Jane Seward, initiated the project over seven years ago as a group activity. With the loving guidance of Jane and Susan, every person present becomes a starmaker. The only rule is that you must make at least one star! "Our youngest starmaker when we started," says Susan, "was my son, Daniel, who was ten."

The stars are collected and assembled into a quilt top by Susan or Jane or sometimes their 83-year-old mother, Martha Babcock. Jane loves to quilt, so she does most of the quilting. "We had such a good time doing this," says Susan, "that every year since, we have made stars on Thanksgiving for a quilt for each in his turn." The quilts are made for the mothers first, then the children, and then the grandchildren.

This starmaking tradition includes the Elliotts; the Sewards; good friends of the Elliotts, the Joyces and the Pinkuses; and Jane and Susan's mother, Martha Babcock. "The quilts represent warm and loving times with family and friends," says Susan, "and are treasured remembrances."

Thanksgiving Star
1984

A host of fabrics, a host of pieces, a host of stars, a host of hands, a host of personalities, and a heap of love are the ingredients found in *Thanksgiving Star*. This quilt is one of the first made by the friends and family members of Tom and Susan Elliott (see story above) as part of their Thanksgiving celebration.

Throughout the year, Susan cuts the diamonds for the six-pointed stars from scrap fabrics, and by Thanksgiving, a box is filled with fabric diamonds that are ripe and ready for piecing. "The fabric scraps range in color and design from the beautiful to the positively horrible," says Susan. Something like 80 to 90 stars are made each Thanksgiving Day, and the rest are made by the person who finishes the top. And Susan adds, "We never rip out stitching, but at times we strengthen it. Nor do we change fabrics that are wrong side up! Every star goes into the quilt as the maker made it." As a result, *Thanksgiving Star* is a cadre of stars that reflect the personalities of their makers.

The starmakers are Tom and Susan Elliott, Elizabeth V. Elliott, Daniel R. Elliott; Richard and Jane Seward, Nettie Jane Seward, Cara Seward; Martha E. Babcock; Reid and Beth R. Joyce, Kathy Joyce, Laurel B. Joyce, Alan Joyce; and Rosa Lynn Brothman Pinkus, Becky Pinkus.

27

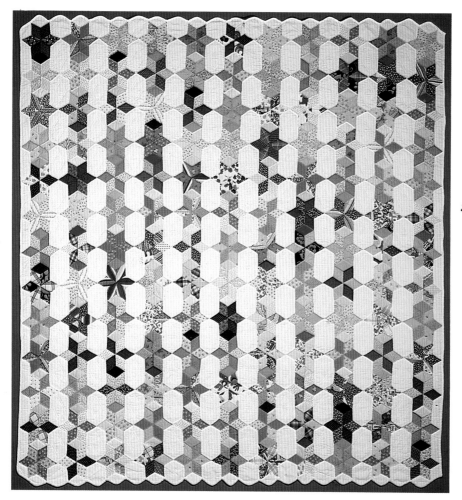

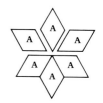

Star Piecing Diagram

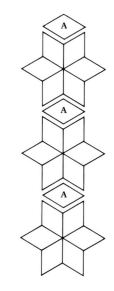

Star Row Piecing Diagram

Thanksgiving Star

Finished Quilt Size
93½″ x 98″

Number of Stars and Finished Size
143 stars—approximately
8½″ x 8½″

Fabric Requirements
Scraps	—5½ yd. total
Solids	—1 yd. total
White	—4¾ yd.
White for bias binding	—1¼ yd.
Backing	—8½ yd.

Number to Cut
Template A	—858 scraps
	132 solids
	26 white
Template B	—120 white
Template C	—20 white
Template D	—24 white

Quilt Top Assembly
1. Join 6 scrap diamonds (A) to form a star, as shown in Star Piecing Diagram. Make 143 stars.
2. Alternate 14 diamonds (A) (12 solids and 2 white) with 13 stars to form a star row, as shown in Star Row Piecing Diagram. Place the white diamond (A) at each end of the row. (See quilt photograph.) Join pieces. Make 11 rows.
3. Join star rows with pieces (B and C), as shown in Setting Diagram. Join pieces (D and A) to quilt edges to complete quilt top, as shown.

Quilting
Outline-quilt ¼″ inside seam line of all pieces. Center diamond template A inside piece B. Use the seam line and cutting line as guides for quilting lines. Mark fabric and quilt.

Finished Edges
Bind quilt with white fabric, pivoting at every corner along quilt edge.

Setting Diagram

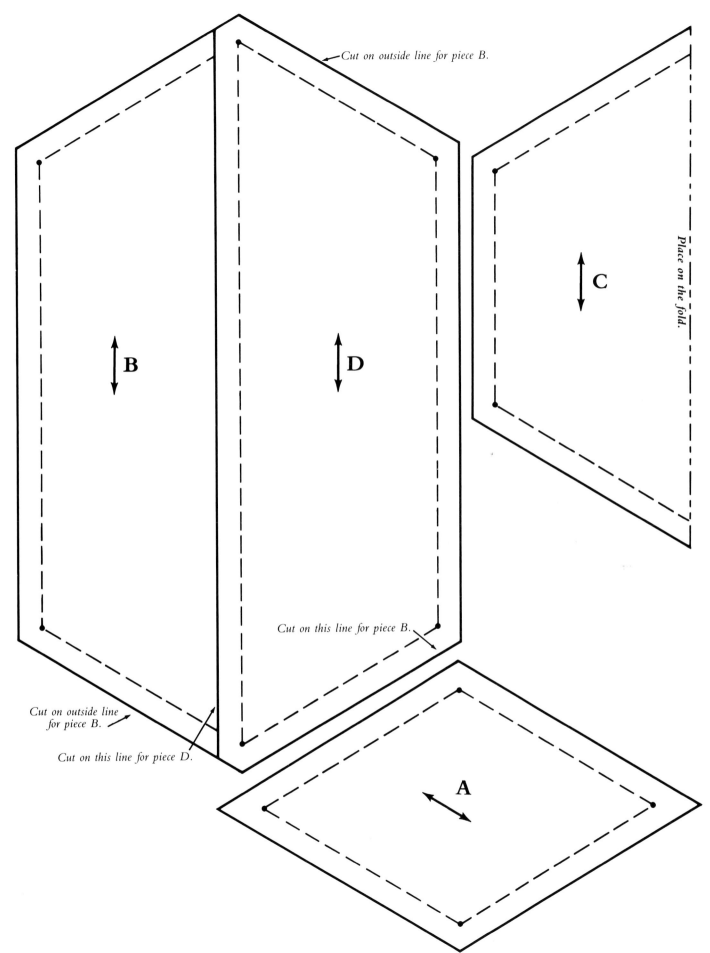

Cut on outside line for piece B.

B

D

C

Place on the fold.

Cut on this line for piece B.

Cut on outside line
for piece B.

Cut on this line for piece D.

A

Elaine is a quilting teacher and lecturer, recognized throughout northern California. Her special love for folding techniques with quilting led to the publication of several booklets, containing the patterns for designs that were favorites among her students. "I prefer to work with dimensional pieces and to design my own patterns," says Elaine, who has a master's degree in home arts.

She is a charter member of her local guild, Ridge Quilters' Guild in Paradise, California, and helped start guilds in two towns nearby. Sometimes feeling isolated in her small town in the foothills in California, Elaine needed something to engage her interest. Now she says, "Quilting has been therapy for me, and designing is my whole life right now."

Elaine De Lancey Shinners

Magalia, California

Folded-Stars Bridal Quilt
1986

The varied textures of crepe satin, netting, and eyelet challenged Elaine to design a quilt that was elegant, eye-appealing, and functional. The result of her efforts, *Folded-Stars Bridal Quilt*, won Best of Show and Best Design at the 1986 Ridge Quilters' Quilt Show in Paradise, California.

Unlike the majority of folded star designs, Elaine's star is folded in a square grid. The square makes this pattern easy to adapt to throw pillows. To anchor folded-star blocks to backing, Elaine used tied quilting (since the blocks should not be quilted). In addition, her borders are attached in a quilt-as-you-go method, because this kind of border seam helps to secure the weight of the folded-star blocks.

Folded-Stars Bridal Quilt

Finished Quilt Size
Approximately 82″ x 96″

Number of Blocks and Finished Size
20 Folded-Star blocks—12″ x 12″

Fabric Requirements
Muslin	— 6¾ yd.
Peach satin	— 2 yd.
Netting	— 3 yd.
Cream eyelet	— 4 yd.
Peach eyelet	— 5 yd.
Floral stripe	— 3¾ yd.
Backing	— 6¾ yd.

Other Materials
2″-wide insertion lace — 19 yd.
Fabric-compatible glue stick
Mercerized crochet thread, peach
Large-eyed embroidery or tapestry
  needle for crochet thread

Number to Cut
Template A	— 100 peach satin
	160 netting
Template B	— 160 cream eyelet
	80 peach eyelet
Template C	— 80 peach eyelet

Quilt Assembly
1. Cut twenty 12½″ squares from muslin. (These will be the backing squares for the folded stars.) Finger-crease or press each square in half twice to form folded-star guidelines. Open square and finger-crease or press each square on the diagonal. Open square and repeat on the opposite diagonal. Open square. There should be a total of 8 guidelines to help with positioning of the folded star.
2. Match centers and align corners of a peach satin square (A) with the guidelines on a muslin square, as shown in Folded-Star Diagram. Anchor peach satin square in place with fabric glue.

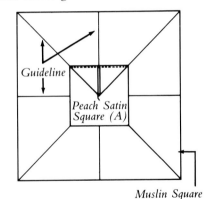

Folded-Star Diagram

3. Fold and press 4 peach satin squares (A) to form folded triangles, as shown in Folding Method #1.

For layer 1 of folded star, place folded triangles at the center of peach satin square anchored in step 2. Match center points of folded triangles with center of peach satin square, as shown in Folded-Star Diagram and block photograph. Tack folded-triangle centers down and baste raw edges in place. Make sure that all edges are straight and that the thread is carried through all layers of fabric.

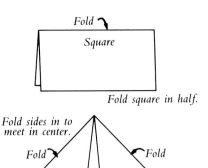

Folding Method #1

4. For layers 2 and 3, fold and press 8 net squares (A), as shown in Folding Method #1. Place a net folded triangle between 2 peach satin folded triangles with point ¾″ from center. (See block photograph.) Align, tack, and baste in place. Repeat three times around.

Place remaining 4 net folded triangles between previously placed net folded triangles in same manner. Align, tack, and baste as before.

5. For layers 4 and 5, fold and press 8 cream eyelet squares (B), as shown in Folding Method #1. Place points of folded triangles 1½″ from center and repeat as done for layers 2 and 3.
6. For layers 6 and 7, fold and press 4 peach eyelet squares (B), as shown in Folding Method #1. Fold and press 4 squares (C) from peach eyelet to form folded squares, as shown in Folding Method #2.

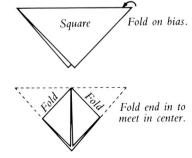

Folding Method #2

Place folded *squares* at corners, with points 2¼″ from center of folded star. (See block photograph.) Tack and baste in place. Center folded triangles on each side, with points 2¼″ from center of folded star. Repeat as done for previous layers.

7. Repeat steps 2 through 6 and complete 20 Folded-Star blocks.

8. Cut 40 block border strips, 1⅝″ x 10¼″, from floral stripe. Center along edge of last layer and join to opposite sides of Folded-Star block. (See block photograph.)

9. Cut 40 block border strips, 1⅝″ x 12½″, from floral stripe. Join in same manner to top and bottom of each block.

10. Cut 16 sashing strips, 3″ x 12½″, from muslin. Cut 16 lengths of 2″ insertion lace. Lay lace strip on muslin sashing strip, center, and stitch to strip.

Alternate 5 Folded-Star blocks (FSB) with 4 sashing strips and join at the tops and bottoms to form a vertical row. (See Setting Diagram.) Make 4 vertical rows.

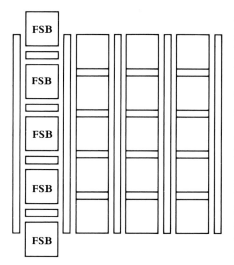

Setting Diagram

11. Cut 5 sashing strips, 3″ wide, from muslin the length of a vertical row. Cut 5 lengths of 2″ insertion lace and sew to muslin strips, as before. Alternate sashing strips with vertical rows and join. (See Setting Diagram.)

12. Cut 2 sashing strips, 3″ wide, from muslin for the top and bottom of quilt. Cut and sew 2″ lace to sashing strips, as before. Join sashing strips to quilt.

13. Cut backing for quilt. Lay backing wrong side up and place batting on top. Center the assembled quilt with right side up over the batting. Smooth it out and pin in place with quilt pins.

Cut forty 8″ lengths of peach crochet thread. Insert threaded needle in folded-star center from front, leaving a 1½″ length of thread in the front. Bring needle from back to front of folded-star center and cut thread, leaving a 1½″ length. Repeat. Tie threads with a square knot in the front. (See block photograph.) Trim threads to an even 1″ length.

Repeat for each Folded-Star block.

14. Cut 2 border strips, 2¾″ wide, from floral stripe for sides of quilt. Cut 2 backing strips, 2¾″ wide, from floral stripe for sides of quilt back. With right sides together, match raw edges of border strip with side of quilt front. Pin or baste in place. With right sides together, match raw edges of backing strip with the same side of quilt back. Pin or baste in place. With one seam, stitch through all five layers (border strip, quilt front, batting, quilt back, and backing strip). Repeat on opposite side of quilt.

Turn border and backing strips so that wrong sides face each other. Insert a strip of batting. Be sure batting is wide enough so that it can be anchored by the seam that joins the next border strip.

15. Cut 2 border strips, 2¾″ wide, from floral stripe for top and bottom of quilt. Cut 2 backing strips, 2¾″ wide, from floral stripe for top and bottom of quilt back. Join to quilt and insert batting in the same manner as in step 14.

16. Cut 2 border strips, 7″ wide, from muslin for sides of quilt. Cut 2 backing strips, 7″ wide, from floral stripe for sides of quilt. Join to quilt and insert batting in the same manner as in step 14.

Machine-quilt down the center of the muslin strip to anchor batting.

17. Cut 2 border strips, 7″ wide, from muslin for top and bottom of quilt. Cut 2 backing strips of each width and length from floral stripe. Join to top and bottom of quilt, insert batting, and machine-quilt as before.

Finished Edges

Cut one hundred thirty-six 4″ squares from muslin for prairie points. Fold each square, as shown in Prairie Point Folding Diagram.

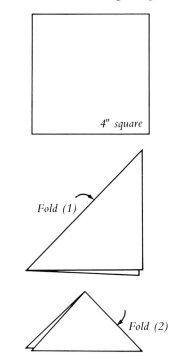

Fold (1)

Fold (2)

Prairie Point Folding Diagram

Arrange prairie points in a continuous, overlapping fashion for sides, top, and bottom, as shown in Prairie Point Arrangement Diagram. Baste prairie points together.

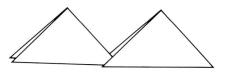

Prairie Point Arrangement Diagram

With raw edges together, stitch prairie points to muslin border strips, as shown in Prairie Point Attachment Diagrams. Turn under raw edge of quilt back to cover raw edges of prairie points and blind-stitch in place.

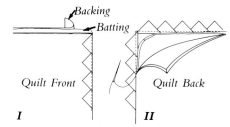

Prairie Point Attachment Diagrams

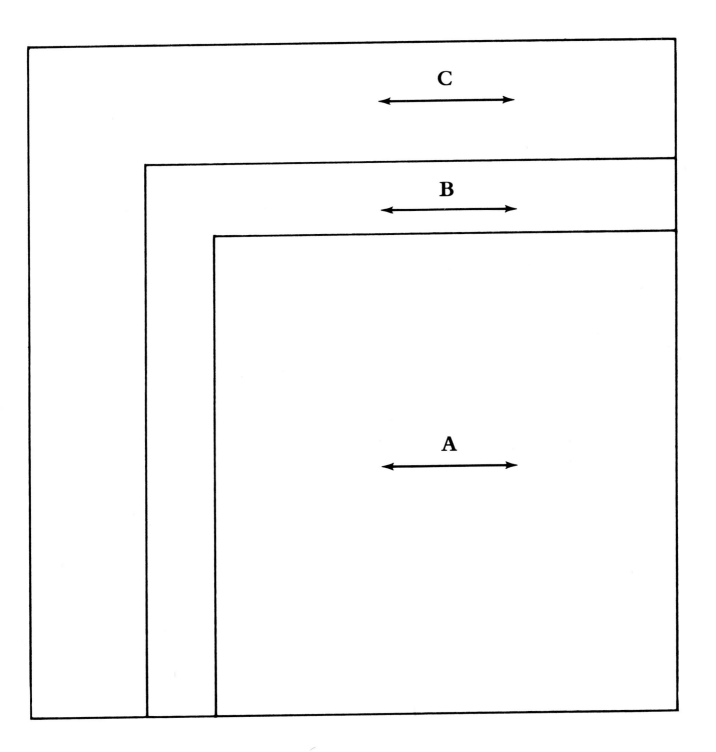

Elizabeth J. Contessa Wuts

Galesbury, Michigan

Elizabeth has mastered machine piecing and machine quilting. Or shall we say Elizabeth is a master at machine piecing and machine quilting? In the short span of three years (short for quilters, that is), she has completed 65 quilts.

From the time her sewing machine needle pierced fabric to make a quilt, Elizabeth knew that this was the way to quilt. Being a speed typist and classical organist, she found that the sewing machine was just another instrument at her fingertips. As a result, she is an enthusiastic supporter of the use of the sewing machine, especially for quilting. "While it is fine to say hand quilting is the traditional way to quilt, it is not necessarily the proper way," says Elizabeth. "Our ancestors quilted by candlelight and oil lamp, but surely no one today would give up the brilliance of modern lighting to squint under candlelight. The analogies are numerous!"

The majority of her quilts are scrap quilts, because they give her the most satisfaction. "I find it fascinating and challenging," says Elizabeth, "to finally produce a work of art out of the dubious-looking remains in my scrap box."

Star-Spangled Banner Scrap Variation

1988

The high contrast between assorted scrap prints and white makes this traditional pattern a vision that vibrates with freshness. Elizabeth's Star-Spangled Banner quilt is one of her many stimulating scrap quilts, completely machine-pieced and machine-quilted, using the quilt-as-you-go method. (Directions are given for both quilt-as-you-go and frame-quilting methods.)

The Star-Spangled Banner block has been around for over a century, but the center panel design is Elizabeth's original.

Star-Spangled Banner Scrap Variation

Finished Quilt Size
78" x 90"

Number of Blocks and Finished Size
6 blocks—28" x 28"

Fabric Requirements
Yellow floral print★ — 2½ yd.
Blue floral print★ — ¾ yd.
Scraps — 2¾ yd. total
White — 5⅓ yd.
Blue for bias
 binding — 1 yd.
Backing — 7¾ yd.★★

★Throughout the directions, yellow floral print and blue floral print will be designated YFP and BFP, respectively.

★★Backing yardage for quilt-as-you-go method is more than yardage needed for frame quilting. Backing yardage for frame quilting is 5¼ yd.

Number to Cut
Template A — 6 YFP
Template B — 792 scraps
 864 white
Template C — 120 scraps
Template D — 56 YFP
 40 BFP
Template E — 1400 scraps
 1400 white
Template F — 24 white
Template G — 24 white
Template H — 108 scraps
 108 white

Quilt Top Assembly

1. Join white triangles (B) to the sides of square (A). Join white triangles (B) to sides of triangles (C) to form small pieced rectangles, as shown in Block Piecing Diagram I. Make 16 small pieced rectangles. Join 4 small pieced rectangles to form a column, as shown in Block Piecing Diagram I. Make 4 columns and join a triangle (C) to one end of each column, as shown.

Join a YFP triangle (D) to each side of 2 columns, as shown, to form pieced triangles. Join the remaining 2 columns to opposite sides of pieced square for center strip, as shown. Join pieced triangles to center strip to form a square.

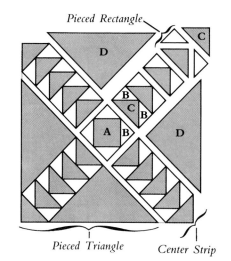

Block Piecing Diagram I

2. Join 36 scrap triangles (E) to 36 white triangles (E) to form pieced squares. Join pieced squares into 2 strips of 8 pieced squares each and 2 strips of 10 pieced squares each, as shown in Block Piecing Diagram II. Join the shorter pieced strips to opposite sides of the square made in step 1, as shown. Join the remaining pieced strips to square, as shown.

Block Piecing Diagram II

3. Refer to Feathered Triangle Piecing Diagram and make 4 feathered triangles with BFP triangles (D), as shown. Join feathered triangles to sides of square made in step 2. (See Block Piecing Diagram III.)

4. Refer to Feathered Triangle Piecing Diagram and make 4 feathered triangles with YFP triangles (D), as shown. Make 4 feathered triangles the mirror image of these, as shown in MI (mirror image) Feathered Triangle Diagram.

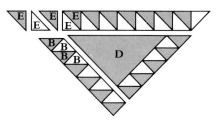

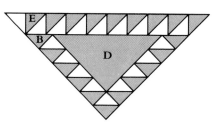

Feathered Triangle Piecing Diagram

MI Feathered Triangle Piecing Diagram

5. Join feathered triangles, made in step 4, to sides of triangle (G) to form a pieced rectangle, as shown in Block Piecing Diagram III. Join 2 pieced rectangles to top and bottom of square, as shown.

Join square (F) to ends of pieced rectangles to form 2 columns, as shown. Join columns to complete Star-Spangled Banner block.

Make 4 blocks as above and 2 blocks reversing the placement of the YFP and BFP triangles (D). (See quilt photograph.)

You have now completed all of the Star-Spangled Banner blocks for this quilt and are ready to machine-quilt. Prepare your blocks for quilting and refer to the first paragraph in the section on quilting. After machine-quilting blocks, continue with step 6. If you are not machine-quilting, continue with step 6.

6. Cut 2 rectangles, 10½" x 7½", from white. Cut 5 squares, 10½" x 10½", from white. Join remaining scrap triangles (E) to remaining white triangles (E) to form pieced squares.

Join pieced squares into columns to join to sides of rectangles and squares, as shown in Center Panel Piecing Diagrams I and II. Before joining pieced squares, note the position of the pieced squares in the diagrams.

Join columns to columns, as shown, before joining to rectangles and squares.

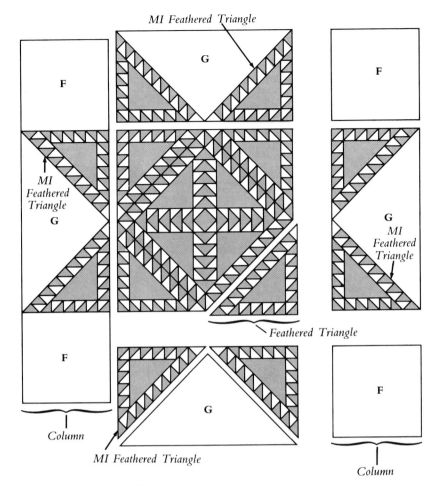

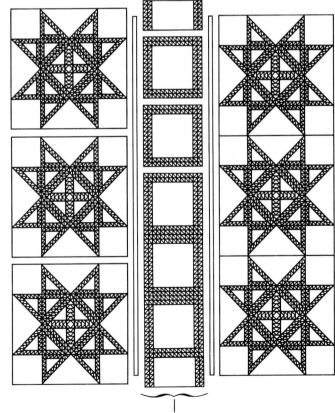

7. Refer to Setting Diagram and join blocks for center panel, as shown.

Cut 2 strips, 1½″ wide, from YFP. Join strips on either side of center panel, as shown in Setting Diagram.

If you are machine-quilting, prepare center panel for quilting and refer to the second paragraph in the section on quilting.

8. Join Star-Spangled Banner blocks in 2 columns of 3 blocks each, as shown in Setting Diagram. Join to sides of center panel.

9. Join scrap triangles (H) to white triangles (H) to form pieced squares. Join pieced squares in 2 columns with 26 pieced squares each, and 2 columns with 28 pieced squares each. (See quilt photograph for pieced square placement.)

If you are machine-quilting, prepare columns for quilting and refer to the last paragraph in the section on quilting.

Join longer columns to sides of quilt and remaining columns to top and bottom of quilt.

Block Piecing Diagram III

Center Panel Piecing Diagram I

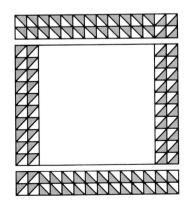

Center Panel Piecing Diagram II

Setting Diagram

37

Quilting

Machine- or hand-quilt each block, as shown in Quilting Diagram. *If you are machine-quilting blocks, return to step 6.*

Elizabeth quilted a feathered wreath in the center of each white square of the center panel. Outline-quilt ¼″ from seam line of all center panel squares and rectangles. Quilt a line ¼″ from that quilting line. Continue in this manner two more times for each center panel square and rectangle. Quilt in-the-ditch of all seam lines that join pieced-square columns. *If you are machine-quilting, return to step 8.* Outline-quilt ¼″ from quilt edge. Quilt a line ¼″ from that line and another ½″ from the first line of quilting. *If you are machine-quilting, return to step 9.*

Finished Edges

Bind with blue fabric.

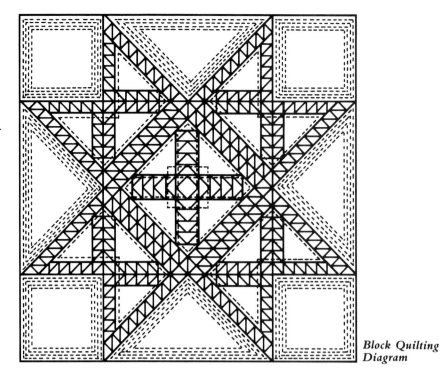

Block Quilting Diagram

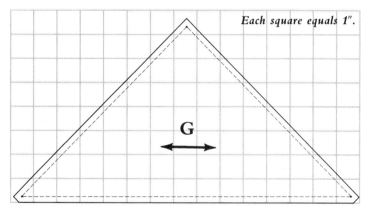

Each square equals 1″.

G

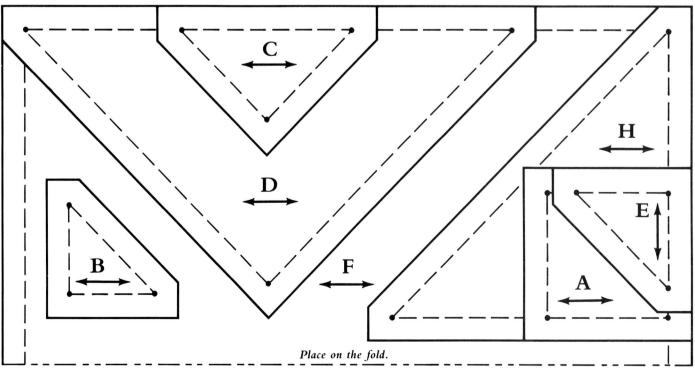

Place on the fold.

Her first and latest stops have been Kansas. Linda has lived in five states and on the island of Okinawa, early in childhood, and later, as an Air Force wife. Born in Kansas, she returned in 1975 with her husband and began her quilting career.

Some 11 years later, she decided to enter her quilts in competitions. During those years of competition, Linda's quilts won over 40 ribbons. "And," says Linda, "I discovered that deadlines were a wonderful incentive for getting quilts done." In 1987 her quilt *Rosemaling Inspiration* was designated as a Masterpiece quilt, which meant she was certified as a Master Quilter by the National Quilting Association. "I felt as if I had won an Olympic gold medal," says Linda.

Discover the variety of quilting techniques Linda capsulized in her quilt, *Persian Paisley*, that is featured in our "Designer Gallery."

Linda Goodmon Emery

Derby, Kansas

Some Are the Same
1988

"Are the stars the same?" That's what everyone asked Linda while she was working on this brown-and-turquoise beauty. Her reply became the name for the quilt— "Some are the same."

Linda's inspiration for making the quilt came from a need to utilize some remnants of simple striped fabrics and zigzag-striped fabrics. "As I progress as a quilter, I am finding a lot of my inspiration for quilts comes from a unique fabric," says Linda, "and it's a challenge to see what I can do with it."

Linda cut the fabric so that the stars would have a kaleidoscope effect. The wide and angular borders adapted well to graceful feather quilting, as well as an original scroll-and-shell quilting pattern by Linda that flowed in and out of every nook and cranny. Linda's hand quilting was so admired by quilters that *Some Are the Same* won the National Quilting Association's Mary Krickbaum Award in 1988 for best execution of hand quilting.

Some Are the Same

Finished Quilt Size
76½" x 90½"

Number of Blocks and Finished Size
20 blocks—14" x 14"

Fabric Requirements
Prints	—1 yd. total★
Stripe I★★	—2¾ yd. ★★★
Stripe II★★	—1 yd.
Stripe III★★	—⅝ yd.
Cream	—1 yd.
Turquoise	—2⅓ yd.
Brown	—3 yd.
Tan for backing	—5¼ yd.

★More yardage may be necessary, depending on the scale and design of the prints.
★★It is possible that one fabric could be found with three different stripes on it. If so, the yardage for one striped fabric is 4½ yd.
★★★Includes yardage for binding.

Number to Cut
Template A	—160 prints
Template B	—160 cream
Template C	—20 stripe I
	40 stripe II
	20 stripe III
Template D	—48 stripe I
	80 turquoise
	80 brown
Template E	—20 stripe I
	40 stripe II
	20 stripe III
Template F	—24 turquoise
	24 brown
Template G	—32 turquoise
Template H	—18 turquoise
Template I	—14 brown

Quilt Top Assembly

1. Referring to Block Piecing Diagrams and colored block drawings, join diamonds (A), triangles (B, C, D, G), and trapezoids (E, F), as shown. Make number of blocks indicated in colored block drawings.

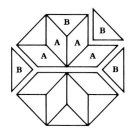

Block Piecing Diagram I

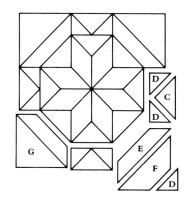

Block Piecing Diagram II
Diagram shows piecing for blocks 1 and 4 only.

turquoise   cream   brown

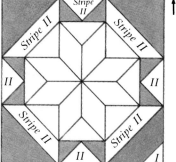

Block 1—Make 2.

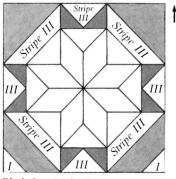

Block 2a—Make 2.

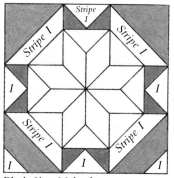

Block 2b—Make 3.

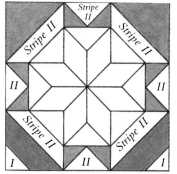

Block 3—Make 5.

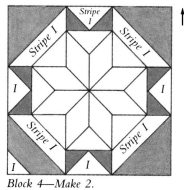

Block 4—Make 2.

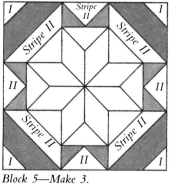

Block 5—Make 3.

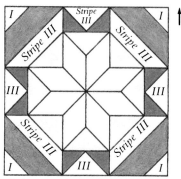

Block 6—Make 3.

2. Arrange blocks, as shown in Block Setting Diagram. Arrows inside the blocks indicate the top of each block. Join blocks at sides and make 5 rows. Join rows.

↑	↑	↑	↑
Block 1	Block 2a	Block 3	Block 4
←	↑	↑	→
Block 2b	Block 5	Block 6	Block 3
←	↑	↑	→
Block 3	Block 6	Block 5	Block 2b
←	↑	↑	→
Block 2b	Block 5	Block 6	Block 3
←	↓	↓	→
Block 1	Block 2a	Block 3	Block 4

Block Setting Diagram

3. Cut 18 strips, 1⅜″ x 10″, from stripe I. Center strip and join to one long side of each of 18 trapezoids (H), as shown in Border Piecing Diagram I.

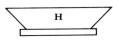

Border Piecing Diagram I

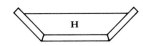

Border Piecing Diagram II

Match stripes with previous strips and cut 28 strips, 1⅜″ wide, from stripe I for short sides of trapezoids (H). Match stripes and join to opposite short sides of 10 trapezoids (H), as shown in Border Piecing Diagram II. Join a strip to one short side of each of the remaining trapezoids, as shown in Border Piecing Diagrams III and IV. These trapezoids will be used at the ends of each border.

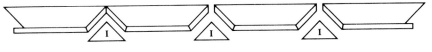

Border Piecing Diagram III

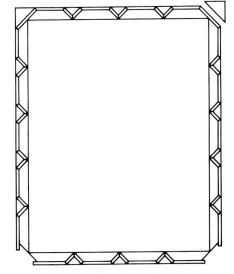

Border Piecing Diagram IV

4. Alternate 4 trapezoids with 3 triangles (I), as shown in Border Piecing Diagram III, and join to form border. Make 2 borders and join to top and bottom of quilt.

Alternate 5 trapezoids with 4 triangles (I) and join. Make 2 borders and join to sides of quilt.

5. Match stripes and cut 4 strips, 1⅜″ wide, from stripe I for corners. Join to quilt, as shown in Border Piecing Diagram IV.

6. Cut 4 right triangles from brown for corners and join to quilt, as shown.

7. Cut 4 borders, 7″ wide, from brown. Join to quilt and miter corners.

Quilting

All of Linda's quilting is done in matching-colored thread. Outline-quilt ¼″ from seam line of triangles in blocks, as shown in Quilting Diagram. Quilt remainder of block, as shown in Quilting Diagram and in quilt photograph. Quilt borders with Linda's original scroll-and-shell design. Background-quilt border with diagonal lines, ½″ apart.

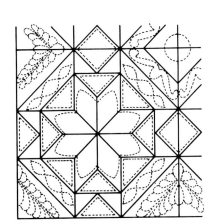

Quilting Diagram

Finished Edges

Bind with 1½″-wide strips of stripe I, matching stripes all around and mitering corners.

Quilt Documentation

Linda cross-stitched her name, date, and quilt title and bordered it with the stripe I fabric used in the quilt. (See photograph of quilt documentation.) The framed documentation is appliquéd to the quilt back. Her name, address, and phone number are printed on muslin and tacked on below (covered in the photograph), which is important to do if your quilt is being shipped somewhere.

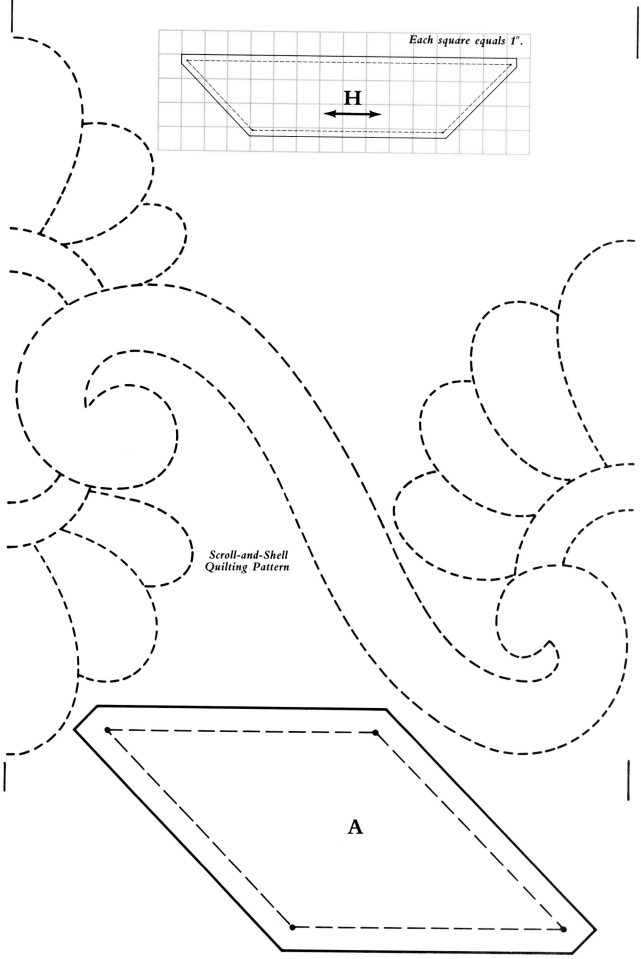

Each square equals 1".

H

*Scroll-and-Shell
Quilting Pattern*

A

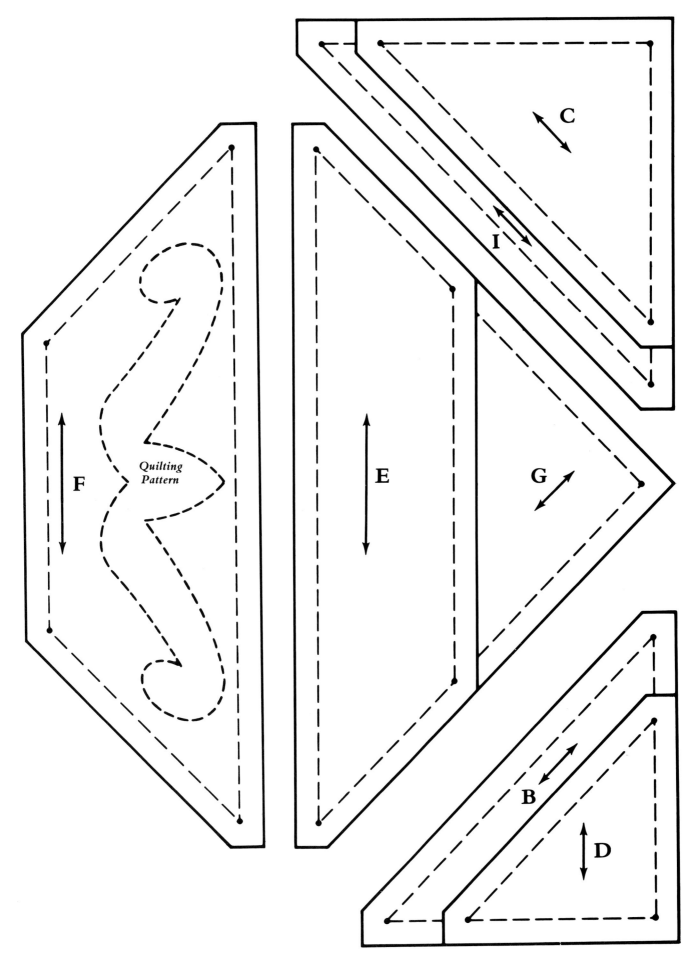

Quilting Pattern

43

Christine Schnaufer

Colona, Illinois

Nestled under the security and warmth of a quilt, with her eyes scanning the expanse of rippled fabric, three-year-old Christine played her made-up game of counting pieces, stitches, and colors to pass the time. That was Christine's first encounter with quilting, and now, as an adult, quilting pacifies her as a quiltmaker, just as her game pacified her as a child. "It is a soothing joy to a hectic mid-life," says Christine.

Though quiltmaking per se entered her life much later, Christine and fabric joined hands that day of the made-up quilt game, and they embarked on numerous adventures. Christine remembers, "I got into trouble once when I cut up dance costumes for doll blankets. And another time, I got into even bigger trouble when I cut apart a yoyo quilt to see how it was made!"

Christine is an active member of the Mississippi Valley Quilters Guild in Davenport, Iowa. "My quilting is for self-expression," says Christine, "and for the romantic notion of carrying on what the women of yesteryear did—to create, to soothe, to warm, to finally sit down!"

Judy's Star Surrounded
1987

It's a whirligig of stars—a whirligig of colors, spinning and tumbling its way into your heart! Christine's scrap star quilt just shouts with joy and makes you smile.

Christine's star block is a modified version of Marsha McCloskey's Twisting Star, which is a variation of the Star of the Orient, designed by Judy Martin. (See "Resources.") Christine added the bars of color to the star and the corner triangles to make a square. As a special touch, she rotated the star blocks so that no two colors would be paired together on the same row. "It makes the quilt move," says Christine. "And because each block was pieced with different fabric, I didn't get bored quilting it."

Judy's Star Surrounded

Finished Quilt Size
70″ x 100″

Number of Blocks and Finished Size
70 blocks—10″ x 10″

Fabric Requirements
Red print   —1½ yd.
Green print   —1½ yd.
Yellow print   —1½ yd.
Orange print   —1½ yd.
Blue print   —1½ yd.
Navy print   —1½ yd.
Lavender print   —1½ yd.
Pink print   —1½ yd.
Lt. scraps   —1¼ yd. total
Dk. scraps   —1¼ yd. total
Muslin   —5 yd.
Backing   —6 yd.

Number to Cut
Template A   —70 muslin★
Template B   —560 muslin★
             280 lt. scraps
             280 dk. scraps
Template C   —70 red print★
             70 green print★
             70 yellow print★
             70 orange print★
             70 blue print★
             70 navy print★
             70 lavender print★
             70 pink print★
Template D   —280 muslin★
★See Finished Edges before cutting fabric.

Quilt Top Assembly
1. Join all lt. scrap triangles (B) and dk. scrap triangles (B) to muslin triangles (B) to form large triangles, as shown in Block Piecing Diagram I. Join them to sides of octagon (A). Begin at one edge of octagon and work to the left, as shown. To join last triangle, stitch up to the intersecting seam line of triangles and octagon. Stop and backstitch 1 or 2 stitches. Remove fabric from the machine. Align the remaining unstitched sides of triangles and stitch from the center to the outside edge.

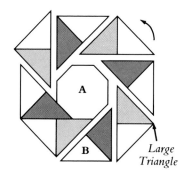

Block Piecing Diagram I

☐ *lt. scraps*   ■ *dk. scraps*

2. Join trapezoids (C) to star, working to the right, as shown in Block Piecing Diagram II. Arrange pieces in the color order shown and join pieces in the same order for every block made.

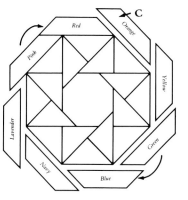

Block Piecing Diagram II

Join triangles (D) to corners of star to complete block, as shown in Block Piecing Diagram III. Make 70 blocks.

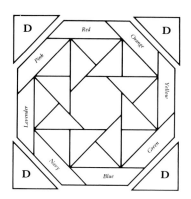

Block Piecing Diagram III

3. Arrange blocks in 10 rows of 7 blocks each. (See quilt photograph.) Christine recommends placing the blocks on the floor or on a sheet to plan color arrangement. "I rotated blocks so that none of the same colors touched," says Christine.

Join blocks at sides to form rows and join rows.

Quilting
Outline-quilt ¼″ inside seam line of all muslin pieces and trapezoids (C).

Finished Edges
To make Christine's pieced bias binding, cut 2 strips each, 3½″ x 51½″, from the same fabrics used for trapezoid C. Cut 1 strip, 3½″ x 51½″, from muslin. Join strips lengthwise in the color order shown in Bias Strip Diagram I to make a 51½″ square. Finger-crease and cut the square in half on its diagonal (bias), as shown in Bias Strip Diagram II.

Muslin (M)	M
Red (R)	R
Orange (O)	O
Yellow (Y)	Y
Green (G)	G
Blue (B)	B
Navy (N)	N
Lavender (L)	L
Pink (P)	P
Red (R)	R
Orange (O)	O
Yellow (Y)	Y
Green (G)	G
Blue (B)	B
Navy (N)	N
Lavender (L)	L
Pink (P)	P

3¼″(3″(3¼″(

51½″ square

Bias Strip Diagram I

Bias Strip Diagram II

Remove long strip of muslin from piece. Leave the small muslin triangle attached. (See Bias Strip Diagram III.) With right sides facing each other, join edges marked Seam 1 with a ¼″ seam to form a parallelogram, as shown in Bias

With right sides facing, match seam lines and colors, and join the edges marked Seam 2 to form a tube, as shown in Bias Strip Diagrams IV and V. Muslin triangle will be left free.

Cut a continuous bias strip, 2½" wide, beginning at the edge with the muslin triangle and going around and around until the whole tube has been used. (See Bias Strip Diagram VI.)

Join bias strip to quilt.

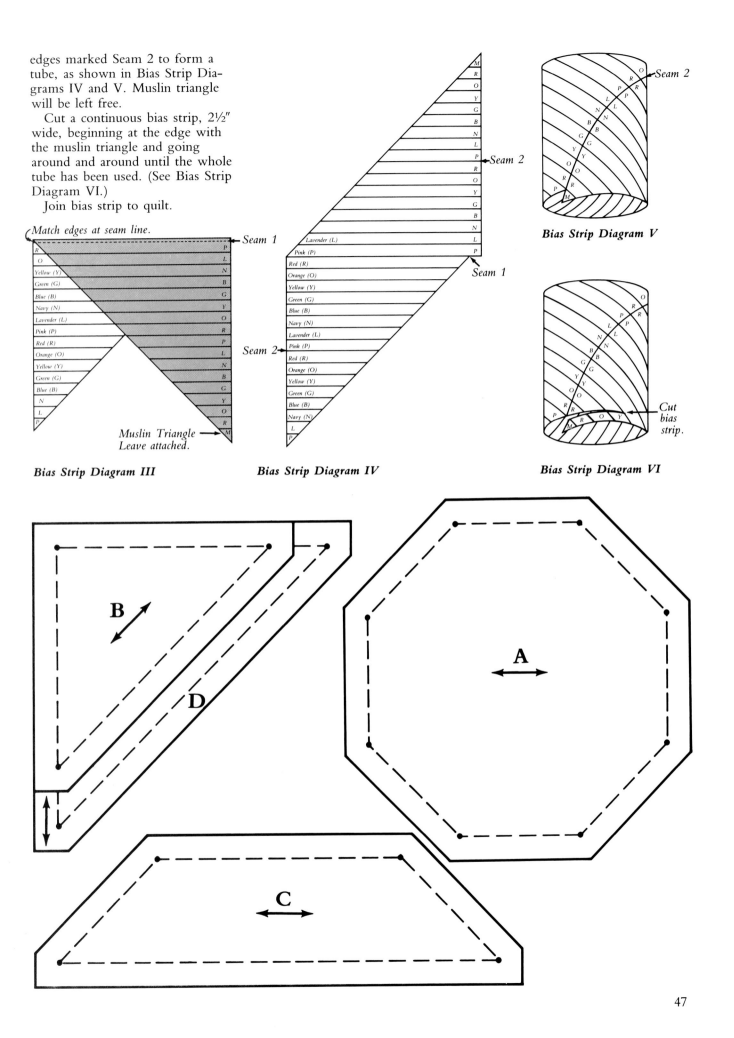

Bias Strip Diagram III

Bias Strip Diagram IV

Bias Strip Diagram V

Bias Strip Diagram VI

Donna Lake
Noti, Oregon

"I think quilting is what I was meant to do," says Donna, who began quiltmaking over 20 years ago. With the assistance of a caring mother-in-law, Donna made her first quilt for her first child in 1962. "It was an appliquéd print bunny with a piece of flannel for the tail," recalls Donna. For a short time after that, Donna maintained that she would only appliqué, because she couldn't imagine cutting fabric into pieces and then sewing them back together. Of course, as you can see, she changed her mind about that. With even a quick observation of Donna's work, one can recognize the expertise that is displayed by her template placement on the fabric and the precision piecing that is required to make the design work.

Turn the pages to our "Quilts Across America" chapter to find *Ribbons 'n Rings*, another example of Donna's forte.

Starry Castle
1988

Careful planning and precise template placement for cutting are the fountainheads that make *Starry Castle* a handsome prototype of the technique so often promoted by Jinny Beyer. Just looking at *Starry Castle*, one has to agree that the incorporation of the prints enhanced the overall design of the quilt and was well worth the time and effort required to achieve it.

Donna's quiltmaking begins with fabric selection. "I usually fall in love with the fabric first," she says. "Then I pick the patterns to go with it." For *Starry Castle*, Donna found that Jinny Beyer's Castle Keep block was perfectly suited to the fabrics she had on hand. (See "Resources" on page 144.)

Before cutting and sewing a quilt, Donna's next step is to make a simple paper-and-fabric mock-up of the block, as shown in the photograph on this page. Fabric pieces are cut without seam allowances for one sample block and glued to paper. Since good-quality print fabrics are expensive, construction of a block mock-up is a good way to save time and money, and to make sure that you are happy with the block before you start.

Donna caps *Starry Castle*'s patchwork geometry with a scroll quilting pattern from Marge Murphy's heirloom quilting designs. (See "Resources.")

Starry Castle

Finished Quilt Size
83″ x 99″

Number of Stars and Finished Size
20 stars—15¾″ x 15¾″
26 small star blocks—6½″ x 6½″

Fabric Requirements
Paisley I★ — 2½ yd.
Paisley II★ — 4½ yd.
Tan print — 3⅞ yd.
Navy/maroon stripe★ — 3 yd.
Dk. maroon print — 2½ yd.
Lt. maroon print — 2½ yd.
Lt. maroon print
for bias binding — 1¼ yd.
Backing — 8½ yd.
★Because of the need to place templates on stripes and paisley swirls, one-half yard has been added to fabric requirements.

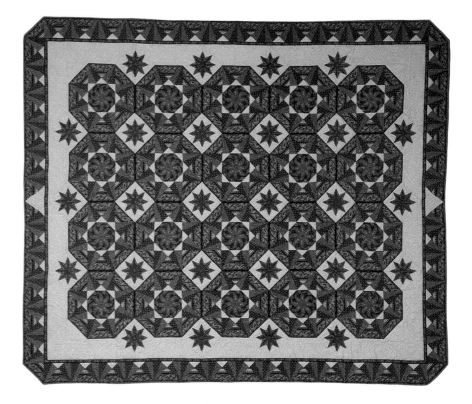

Number to Cut
Template A★★ — 212 paisley II
Template B — 260 dk. maroon print
Template B★★★ — 260 lt. maroon print
Template C — 212 tan print
Template D★★ — 160 paisley I
Template E★★ — 208 navy/maroon stripe
Template F — 104 tan print
Template F★★★ — 104 tan print
Template G — 18 tan print
Template H — 4 tan print
Template I — 2 tan print
Template J — 2 paisley II
Template J★★★ — 2 paisley II
★★See photograph of quilt before cutting fabric. Using the two-mirror technique may also be helpful with template placement. (See Editor's Note, page 6.)
★★★Flip or turn over template if fabric is one-sided.

Quilt Top Assembly

1. Join 8 triangles (D) at sides, as shown in Star Block Piecing Diagram. Join 4 triangles (C) to sides to form a square, as shown.

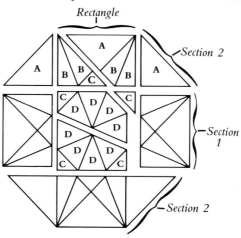

Star Piecing Diagram

Join light and dark maroon triangles (B) at longest edge, twice, as shown. Join triangle (C) to one set of triangle Bs. Join triangle (A) to the other set of triangle Bs, as shown. Join pieces to form a rectangle. Make 4. Join two of them to the opposite sides of center square (section 1). Join triangles (A) to the opposite sides of the remaining two (section 2). Join sections, as shown, to complete star. Make 20 stars.

2. Join 8 diamonds (E) at sides, as shown in Small Star Block Piecing Diagrams. Join piece (F) to sides of star to form a square. Make 26 small star blocks.

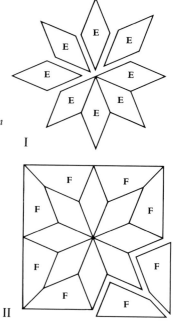

Small Star Block Piecing Diagrams

3. Alternate small star blocks (SB) with stars (S) to form diagonal rows, as shown in Setting Diagram I. Join rows.

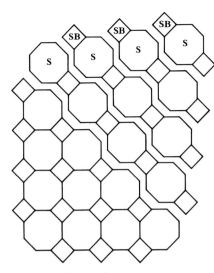

Setting Diagram I

4. Join pieces (G) to sides, top, and bottom of quilt, as shown in Setting Diagram II.

Join pieces (G) to the opposite sides of piece (H) to form corner section, as shown in Setting Diagram II. Make 4 corner sections and join to quilt.

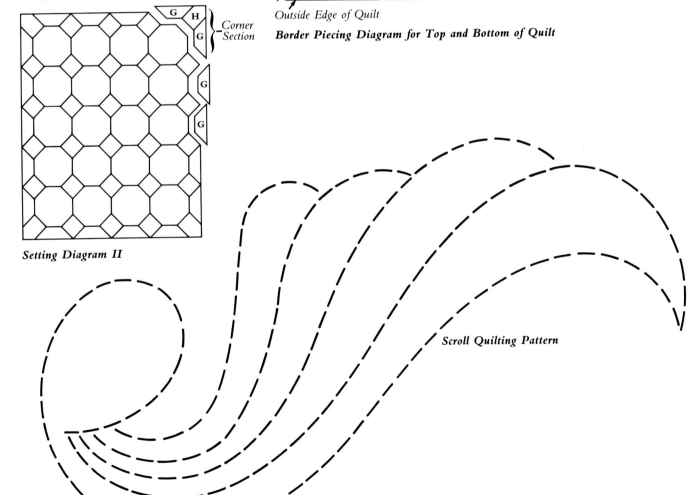

Setting Diagram II

5. Cut 4 border strips, 1¼″ wide, following stripe of navy/maroon print fabric. Join to quilt and miter corners.

6. Join pieces (A, B, and C), as done for stars, to form border rectangles. Make 48. Join 14 rectangles at sides to form one pieced border for quilt side. Make one more border and join borders to quilt sides.

7. Join pieces (B, C, I, and J) to form center border rectangle, as shown in Border Piecing Diagram for Top and Bottom of Quilt. Make 2 rectangles.

Join 5 border rectangles, made in step 6, at sides for pieced border for top and bottom of quilt. Make 4. Join pieced borders to opposite sides of center border rectangle, as shown in Border Piecing Diagram for Top and Bottom of Quilt. Make 2 pieced borders.

Join triangle (A) to each end of pieced border. (See quilt photograph.) Join borders to top and bottom of quilt.

Quilting
Outline-quilt ¼″ inside seam lines of stars, small star blocks, and pieced borders. Donna followed the paisley pattern of her fabric and quilted it for accent. Quilt scroll pattern on tan print pieces G and H. (See quilt photograph.)

Finished Edges
Bind with lt. maroon print fabric.

Border Rectangle *Center Border Rectangle*

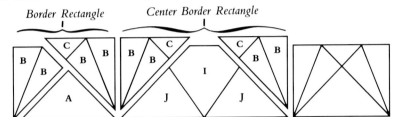

Outside Edge of Quilt

Border Piecing Diagram for Top and Bottom of Quilt

Scroll Quilting Pattern

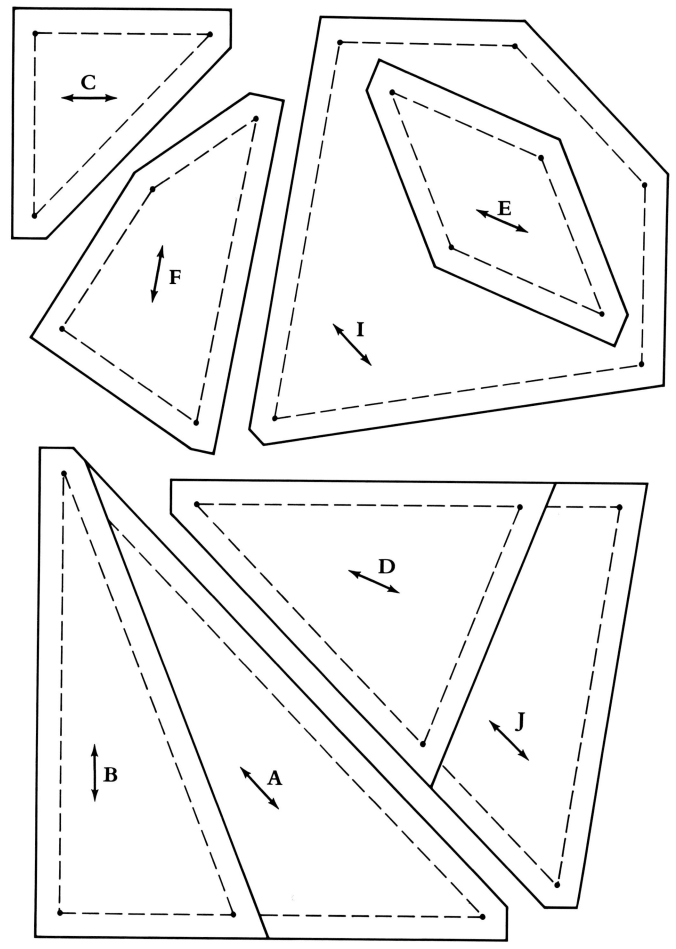

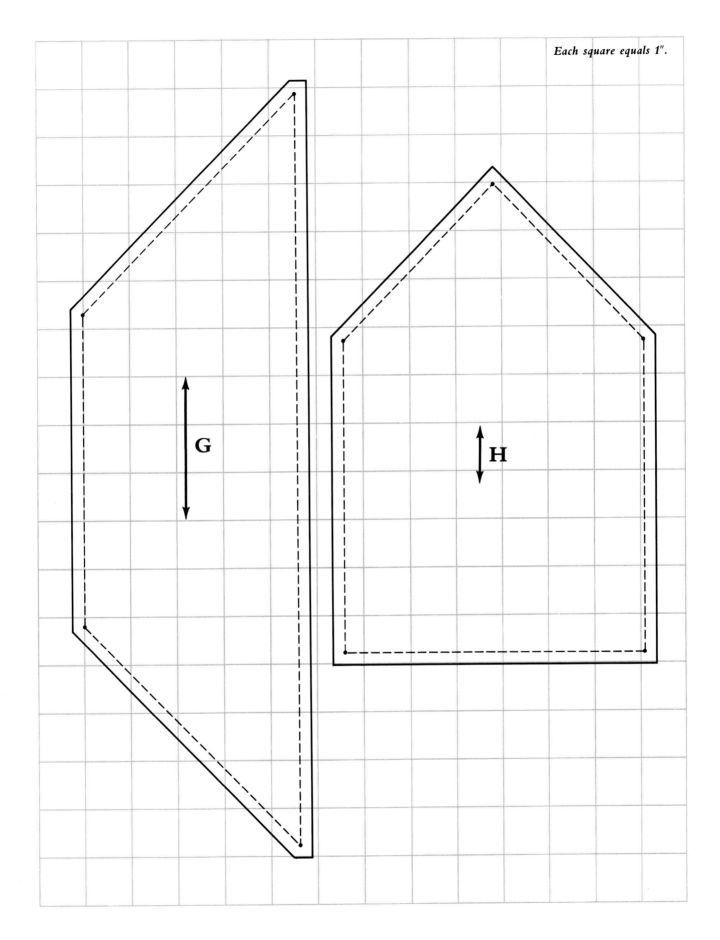

G

H

Pauline Spieks

Stone Mountain, Georgia

This native Tennessean and only girl out of four children has had a fancy for needlework since she was 12 years old. Sewing and needlework were her pride and glory as a young girl, and she has the blue ribbons to prove it.

In 1929 she began making quilts, first for the family and later for her husband and children. For most of her married life, quiltmaking was delayed by the need to make clothes for her children and to produce income by making draperies and bridal clothes for others. In 1981 the opportunity crossed her path once again to pick up a needle and quilt. Encouraged by a good friend, Anne Oliver, Pauline threw her energies into quilting. "It started me in a new way of life," says Pauline. "I am still going strong. I don't need much sleep," she says, "so I am planning all the time."

Featured in our "Quilts Across America" chapter is another of Pauline's quilted treasures, *Williamsburg Palm*.

Star and Crescent
1984

Precision, precision, precision— that's what makes Pauline's *Star and Crescent* a first-rate quilt. And Pauline will be the first person to tell you that to attain that precision took practice and patience. "My first block for *Star and Crescent* did not turn out very well," says Pauline. From that experience she learned that each piece had to be cut to exact measurements, and all points marked. As she progressed with her piecing, she recalls, "My iron became my best friend." Says Pauline, "I used my water sprayer to make the seams lie very flat.

Then I trimmed them to ⅛", misted them again, and pressed them to the dark side." The practice and patience paid off when Pauline and *Star and Crescent* were featured in an article in *Quilt* magazine some months later. (See "Resources.")

Pauline's friend, Anne Oliver, assisted Pauline with the quilting pattern. "I give thanks to my very dear friend, Anne," says Pauline. "She is a very good pusher." Recalls Pauline, "Anne would say to me, you can do it!" Aren't we glad that Pauline had Anne to encourage her.

Star and Crescent

Finished Quilt Size
102" x 117"

Number of Blocks and Finished Size
42 blocks—15" x 15"

Fabric Requirements
Red print — 6½ yd.
Muslin — 12¼ yd.
Red print for
  bias binding — 1¼ yd.
Backing — 10 yd.

Number to Cut
Template A — 168 red print
Template B — 168 muslin
Template C — 168 red print
Template D — 168 muslin
Template E — 78 red print
Template F — 4 red print
Template G — 82 red print

Quilt Top Assembly

1. Join piece (B) to piece (C) to form a pieced cone, as shown in Block Piecing Diagram. Make 4. Alternate cones with diamonds (A) and join at sides, as shown. Join pieces (D), as shown, to complete block. Make 42 blocks.

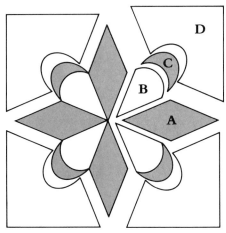

Block Piecing Diagram

2. Join 6 blocks at sides to form a row. Make 7 rows and join rows.
3. Cut 4 borders, 6½" wide, from muslin. Join to quilt and miter corners.
4. Appliqué scallops (E and F) to borders, as shown in quilt photograph. Appliqué circle (G) at the point where scallops meet.

Quilting

Outline-quilt outside seam line of pieces (A and C). Quilt scroll-and-circle pattern in block corners. (See quilt photograph.)

Finished Edges

Bind with red print fabric.

B

Half of Design

*Scroll-and-Circle
Quilting Pattern*

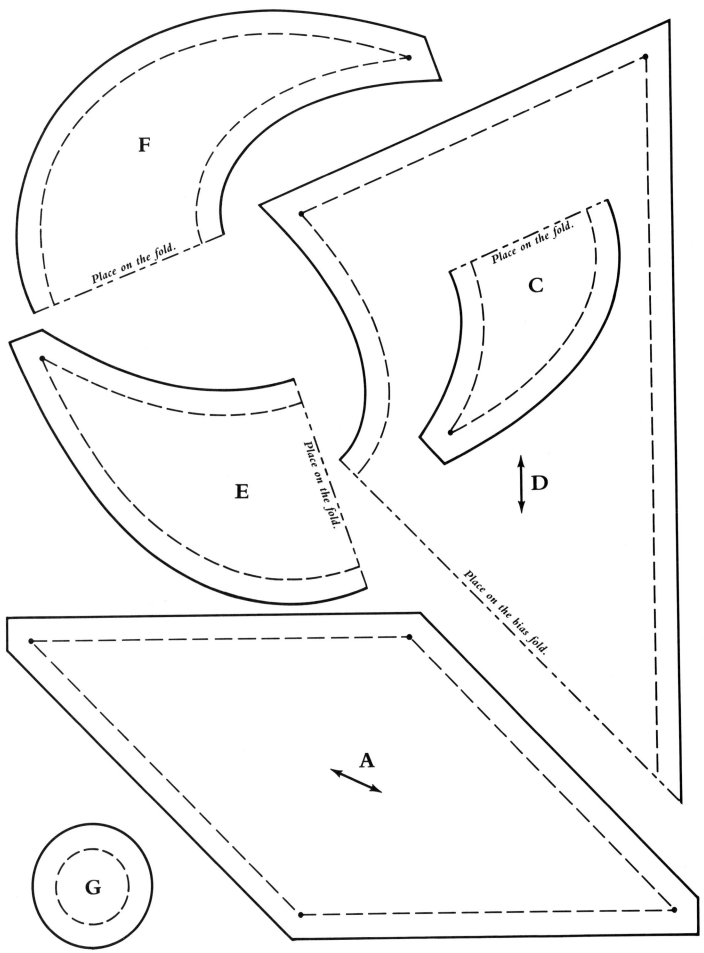

F

Place on the fold.

C

Place on the fold.

D

E

Place on the fold.

Place on the bias fold.

A

G

57

Susan Craig Campbell

Flint, Texas

One stitch at a time—that's how Susan's uniform quilting stitches are made. "I've probably been called crazy for doing it that way," says Susan, "but the stitching is the first thing that people notice about my quilts." Susan has found that this quilting technique gives her the effect that she wants. "It looks as if each stitch just punches through the layers," says Susan, "and suddenly, a flat quilt top takes shape with a beautiful puffed-up design."

Her B.S. degree in clothing and textiles provided the background for her love of handwork. When she made garments for various clothing classes, unlike her fellow students, she found that the handwork, whether basting or hemming, was the most satisfying. "With that attitude toward handwork," says Susan, "quilting fits me to a T!"

Starflower
1985

Whether you call them starflowers, peonies, lilies, or poinsettias, the pieced flowers in this quilt block continue to charm multitudes of quilters. Through the years the stems and leaves have been twisted and turned, straightened and pruned to create a spark of uniqueness. Yet, with each twist and turn, the flowers remain unflappable and maintain their radiant appeal, despite the engineering below.

Susan made *Starflower* as an heirloom quilt for her daughter. It won many ribbons the year it was made. Among them were the Best of Show ribbon at the Quilter's Guild of East Texas Show, Tyler, Texas, and the Best of Show and First Place ribbons at Annie Needlecraft Fair, Big Sandy, Texas, in 1985.

ings at seam lines of green diamonds and stitch seams closed.

Join triangles (E) to pieces (D) to complete blocks.

3. Set Starflower blocks (S) on the diagonal and alternate with muslin squares and right triangles, as shown in Setting Diagram. Join to form 8 diagonal rows. Join rows and remaining corner triangles.

4. Cut 4 borders, 2½″ wide, from rust. Join to quilt and miter corners.

5. Cut 4 borders, 3″ wide, from muslin. Join to quilt and miter corners.

6. Cut 4 borders, 4¼″ wide, from rust. Join to quilt and miter corners.

Starflower

Finished Quilt Size
85″ x 102″

Number of Blocks and Finished Size
20 Starflower blocks—12″ x 12″

Fabric Requirements
Rust	—3 yd.
Rust print	—2⅛ yd.
Green★	—2½ yd.
Muslin	—5¾ yd.
Rust print for bias binding	—1¼ yd.
Backing	—8¾ yd.

★Set aside 1¼ yd. to make bias strips for stems.

Number to Cut
Template A	—360 rust print
	120 green
Template B	—240 muslin
Template C	—240 muslin
Template D	—20 muslin
Template E	—20 green
Template F	—20 green
Template G	—20 green
12½″ squares	—12 muslin
Right triangles	—14 muslin with 12″ finished *sides*
	4 muslin with 12″ finished bias (hypotenuse)

Quilt Top Assembly
1. Join sides of 6 rust print diamonds (A), and 2 green diamonds (A), as shown in Starflower Piecing

Diagram. Stitch all seams *from* and *to* seam lines. Make 3 starflowers.

Starflower Piecing Diagram

Set squares (B) and triangles (C) between diamonds, as shown in Starflower Block Piecing Diagram.

When joining square B between the *green* diamonds, leave an unstitched portion wide enough to insert the ends of the appliquéd stems. (See Starflower Block Piecing Diagram.)

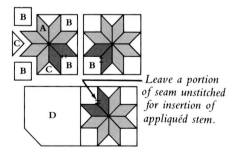

Leave a portion of seam unstitched for insertion of appliquéd stem.

Starflower Block Piecing Diagram

Join pieced squares and piece (D) at sides to form 2 rows, as shown in Starflower Block Piecing Diagram. Join rows. Make 20.

2. Cut bias strips for stems, 1″ wide (includes seam allowance), from green. Mark blocks using stem guide. Appliqué stems and leaves (F and G). Insert stems through open-

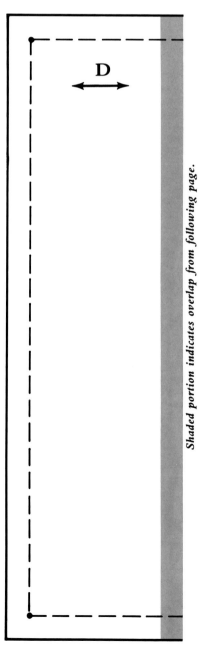

Shaded portion indicates overlap from following page.

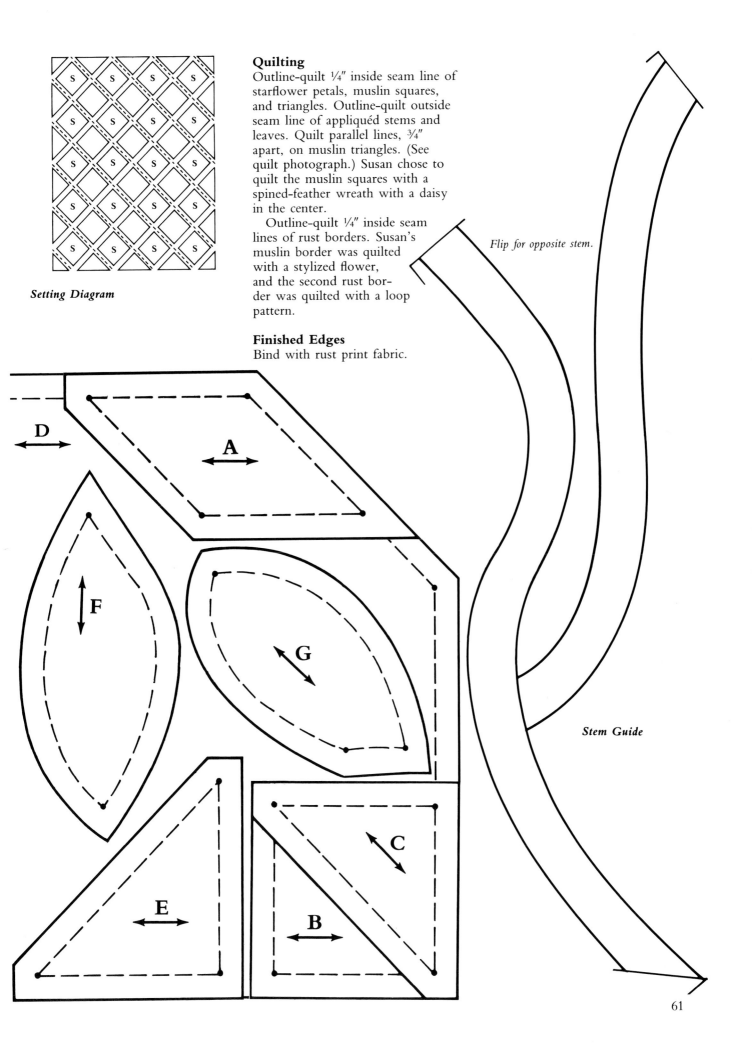

Setting Diagram

Quilting

Outline-quilt ¼″ inside seam line of starflower petals, muslin squares, and triangles. Outline-quilt outside seam line of appliquéd stems and leaves. Quilt parallel lines, ¾″ apart, on muslin triangles. (See quilt photograph.) Susan chose to quilt the muslin squares with a spined-feather wreath with a daisy in the center.

Outline-quilt ¼″ inside seam lines of rust borders. Susan's muslin border was quilted with a stylized flower, and the second rust border was quilted with a loop pattern.

Finished Edges

Bind with rust print fabric.

Flip for opposite stem.

D

A

F

G

Stem Guide

E

C

B

QUILTS
ACROSS
AMERICA

Carol Doak

Windham, New Hampshire

Carol's initial purpose for learning to quilt was to make use of an abundance of sewing scraps. "I began to quilt with no idea how important it would become to me," says Carol. In a short time Carol's quilts adorned the beds and walls throughout her house, confirming the pleasure Carol reaped from quilting.

Another aspect of quilting that has caused it to retain its appeal for Carol is the friendship factor. Carol expresses it best when she says, "I used to rationalize that it was the quilts that attracted individuals of all ages who appreciate, share, and give so much of themselves, but now I believe that the quilts are just the means to the end. No other art form or craft has such a support network," says Carol. As a quilt teacher, Carol has observed that most individuals become involved with quilting because of the quilts but continue because of the quilters.

Carol is a member of the Hannah Dustin Quilter's Guild of Hudson, New Hampshire, and the New England Quilter's Guild of Lowell, Massachusetts. Carol's quilts have won various ribbons, including several for best of show, from both state and national quilt competitions.

Comical Country
1987

Old MacDonald never had a farm quite like this one. There's a mischief-maker in every pen, in the orchard, and in the flower bed. Can you find them?

Comical Country won the Best of Show ribbon at the New England Quilter's Guild Show, Fall 1987. "I love to see the smiles that this quilt elicits from both young and old," says Carol.

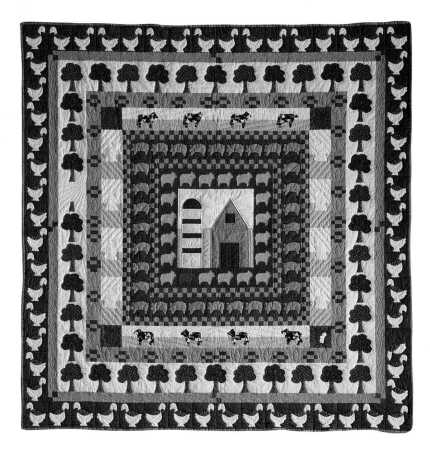

Comical Country

Finished Quilt Size
80" x 80"

Fabric Requirements
Green — 2½ yd.
Lt. blue/green — ¾ yd.
Dk. green print I — ⅝ yd.
Dk. green print II — ⅝ yd.
Dk. teal — ¾ yd.
Pink (pig) — ¾ yd.
Beige print I
  (rabbit) — ⅜ yd.
Beige print II
  (duck) — 1⅜ yd.
Lt. beige print — ⅓ yd.
Lt. brown — ½ yd.
Dk. brown — ½ yd.
Dk. brown print — ½ yd.
Lt. blue — 2¼ yd.
Blue calico — ½ yd.
Red — ¾ yd.
Gray — 3 yd.★
Gray print (sheep) — ½ yd.
Black — ⅛ yd.
White — ⅛ yd.
Black/white
  print (cow) — ⅜ yd.
Backing★★ — 4⅝ yd.
★Includes yardage for bias
binding.
★★See note in Quilting before
purchasing fabric.

Other Materials
Freezer paper
Fabric-compatible glue stick

Number To Cut
Template A — 2 lt. blue/green
              1 lt. blue
Template B — 2 lt. brown
              2 dk. brown
Template C — 1 lt. brown
Template D — 1 lt. brown
Template E — 1 dk. brown
Template F — 1 lt. brown
Template F★★★ — 1 lt. brown
Template G — 1 lt. brown
Template H — 1 lt. blue
Template I★★★ — 1 lt. blue
Template J — 1 lt. blue/green
Template K — 1 lt. blue
              20 red‡
              32 green‡
              4 dk. teal‡
Template L — 1 lt. beige print
Template M — 3 dk. brown
Template N — 3 lt. beige print
Template O — 1 dk. brown
Template P‡ — 19 gray print
              1 black
Template Q‡ — 31 pink
Template Q★★★/‡ — 1 pink
Template R★★★/‡ — 4 black/white
                    print
Template R‡ — 4 black/white
              print

Template S — 3 red
Template T — 1 red
Template U — 1 white
Template V — 8 green
Template W — 3 beige print I
Template W★★★ — 4 beige print I
Template X — 1 beige print I
Template Y — 32 gray
Template Z‡ — 40 lt. blue
Template AA — 39 dk. brown
                print
Template BB‡ — 1 dk. brown
                print
Template CC — 20 dk. green
                print I
              19 dk. green
                print II
Template DD‡ — 60 green
Template EE★★★ — 30 beige print II
Template EE — 29 beige print II
Template FF — 1 beige print II
Template GG★★★ — 30 blue calico
Template GG — 29 blue calico
Template HH — 1 blue calico
★★★Flip or turn over template if
fabric is one-sided.
‡ See steps 2, 5, 7, 9, 13, and 15
before cutting fabric.

Quilt Top Assembly
1. Referring to photograph of center block and Center Block Piecing Diagrams, join pieces as shown. Appliqué piece O to square K before joining.

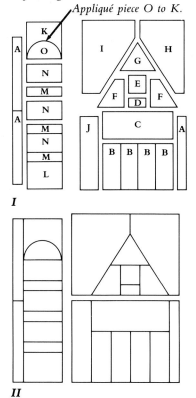

Center Block Piecing Diagrams

2. For sheep blocks, use rotary cutter to cut three 5"-wide strips of red. Cut strips into twenty 5" squares.

Trace 20 sheep (P) *without* seam allowance on dull side of freezer paper. Cut out on traced line. Iron 19 sheep, shiny side down, to wrong side of gray print fabric and 1 sheep to black fabric along lengthwise or crosswise grain of fabric. Cut fabric out, leaving a 1/4" seam allowance. Turn seam allowance to back of paper and stick down with fabric glue, clipping seam allowance at indentations and curves.

Center sheep on red square and appliqué. Cut fabric from behind sheep and remove freezer paper.

Place template K over appliquéd sheep so that the sheep is in the center of the square. Mark cutting line and trim fabric. Carol found that appliquéing to an oversized square allowed her the room to make sure that each item was uniformly placed and straight on each square.

3. Join 4 sheep blocks at tops and bottoms, twice, and join to center block sides, as shown in Sheep Border Setting Diagram. Join 6 sheep blocks at sides, twice. Refer to Sheep Border Setting Diagram for placement of black sheep. Join to top and bottom of center block.

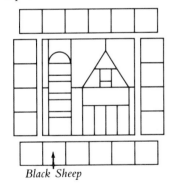

Black Sheep

Sheep Border Setting Diagram

4. For checkerboard, cut 11 strips, 1 1/2" wide, each from dk. teal and gray on the crosswise grain. Sew a dk. teal strip to a gray strip with a lengthwise seam. Cut across strips at 1 1/2" intervals. Alternate colors and join segments to form checkerboard. Refer to quilt photograph and join the appropriate number of segments for each checkerboard border. Notice eight four-patch checkerboard squares are used in

the next to the last border.

Join first checkerboard border, as shown in Checkerboard Setting Diagram.

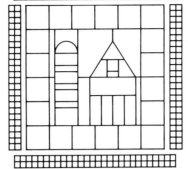

Checkerboard Setting Diagram

5. Follow the same method that was used in step 2 and appliqué pigs (Q) to thirty-two 5" squares of green. (One pig will be facing the wrong way.) Use template K, as before, and trim fabric.

Join 7 pig blocks at tops and bottoms, twice. Refer to quilt photograph for the placement of the one pig that is facing the wrong way. Join 9 pig blocks at sides, twice. Join to quilt as before.

6. Refer to quilt photograph and join checkerboard border to quilt, as before.

7. Cut 2 strips, 2 1/2" wide, each on the crosswise grain, from lt. blue/green and lt. blue. Join lt. blue/green strips to lt. blue strips with a lengthwise seam. Cut across strips at 10 1/2" intervals.

Prepare cows (R) for appliquéing, as before. Center 7 cows on 10 1/2" strips and appliqué. Place one cow off-center and appliqué.

8. Cut 1 strip, 5 1/2" wide, each on the crosswise grain from lt. blue/green and lt. blue. Join strips with a lengthwise seam. Cut across strips at 4 1/2" intervals.

Prepare rabbits (W and X) for appliquéing, as before. Refer to quilt photograph for placement of rabbits and appliqué to lt. blue/green-lt. blue rectangles.

9. Cut four 5" squares from dk. teal. Prepare apples (S and T), leaves (V), and core (U) for appliquéing. Refer to quilt photograph and center apples on squares and appliqué. Place template K over apple square so that apple is centered. Mark cutting line and trim fabric.

10. Arrange and join cow, rabbit, and apple blocks into strips, as shown in quilt photograph. Join to quilt as before.

11. Cut strips, 1 1/4" wide, on the crosswise grain of fabric as follows:

Fabric	Number to Cut
Gray	5
Pink	7
Green	5
Red	2

Join strips with a lengthwise seam as follows: gray, pink, green, gray. Make 2 sets. Make another set at least 20" in length. Press seams down and cut sets at 1 1/4" intervals.

Join strips with a lengthwise seam as follows: pink, red, pink, green. Make 2 sets. Press seams up and cut sets at 2" intervals.

Join 1 1/4" and 2" segments, as shown in Posy Piecing Diagram. Make 35. Make 1 replacing red with pink and pink with red.

gray	*pink*	*gray*
pink	*red*	*pink*
green	*pink*	*green*
gray	*green*	*gray*

Posy Piecing Diagram

12. Alternate posy blocks with gray squares (Y) and join at sides to form strips. (See quilt photograph.) Join to quilt as before.

13. Cut 7 strips, 7" wide, on the crosswise grain of lt. blue fabric. Cut across strips at 7" intervals.

Prepare tree trunks (AA and BB) and tree branches (CC) for appliquéing, as before. Center on lt. blue squares. As Carol puts it, "One tree died so they had to cut it down."

Place template Z over square so that tree is centered. Mark cutting lines and trim fabric. The tree stump should be centered at the bottom edge of the square. (See quilt photograph.)

Join tree blocks to form strips, and join to quilt, as before.

14. Cut 8 borders, 2 1/2" wide, from gray. Alternate with checkerboard squares, as shown in quilt photograph and join to quilt.

15. Cut 9 strips, 6″ wide, on the crosswise grain of the fabric from green. Cut strips at intervals of 6″.

Prepare ducks (EE and FF) and shawls (GG and HH) for appliquéing, as before. Center ducks on green squares and appliqué. Appliqué shawls to ducks.

Alternate ducks facing left with ducks facing right and refer to quilt photograph for placement of the nosy duck. Place template DD over duck square so that duck is centered. Mark cutting line and trim fabric. Join blocks to form strips and join to quilt.

Quilting

Carol used quilting thread to match the colors of the fabrics whenever possible. For this reason, she decided to use a busy backing fabric, on which all the thread color changes would not be noticed. Outline-quilt ¼″ inside seam line of center block pieces, red blocks, checkerboard borders, center rectangle of posies. Sheep are quilted inside in a spiral, with lines about ¼″ apart, to give a textured look. Outline-quilt outside appliquéd seam line of pigs, trees, and ducks. Rabbit blocks are background-quilted

with opposing diagonal lines, 1″ apart. (See quilt photograph.) Quilt Carol's tulip pattern in solid gray blocks of posy border. The solid gray border is quilted in a leaf-and-vine pattern. A crescent shape is quilted just below the shawl of each duck to simulate the wing.

Finished Edge

Bind with gray fabric.

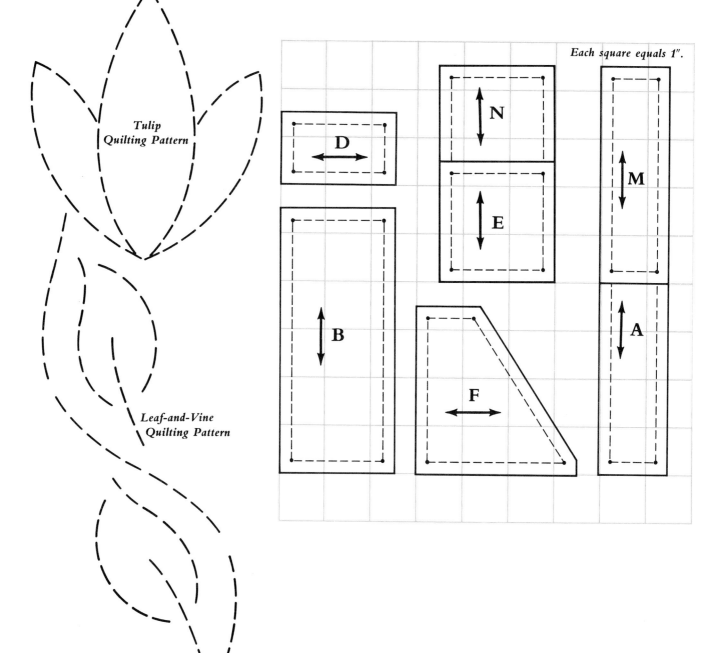

Tulip Quilting Pattern

Leaf-and-Vine Quilting Pattern

Each square equals 1″.

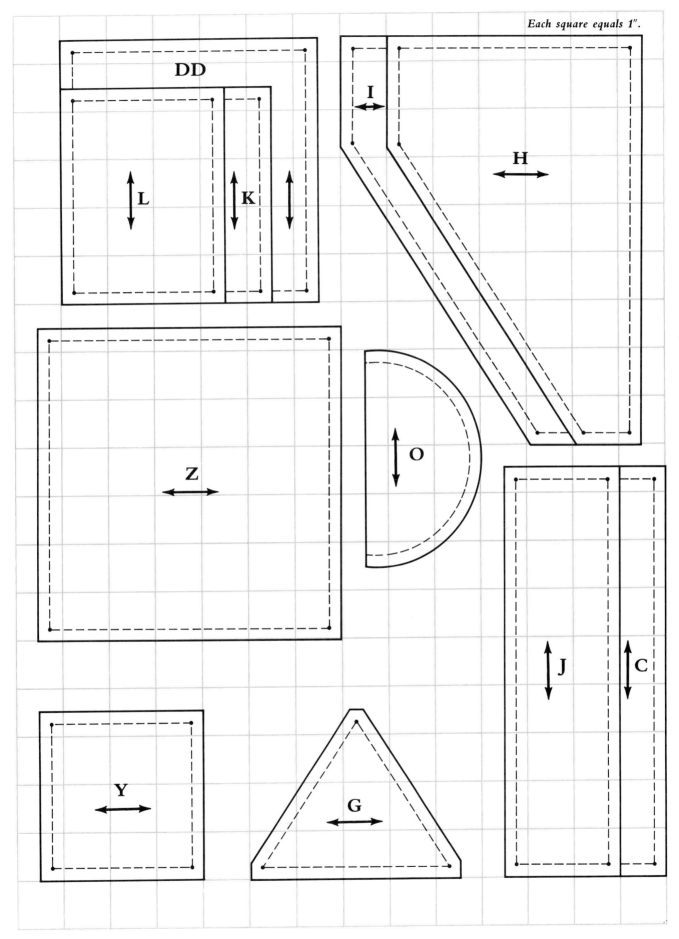

Each square equals 1″.

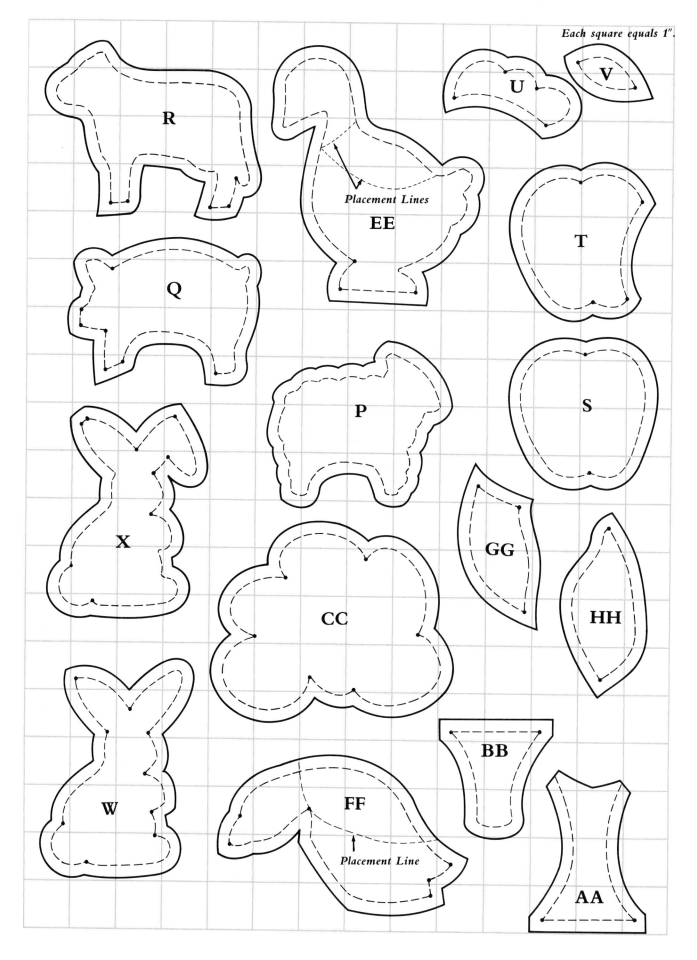

Each square equals 1".

R

EE

Placement Lines

U

V

T

Q

P

S

X

CC

GG

HH

W

FF

Placement Line

BB

AA

The more difficult the pattern for piecing a quilt, the better Michaeline likes it. "I enjoy the challenge of figuring out how to put something together and making it work," says Michaeline. And for patterns with lots of points and intersections, she prefers the accuracy and ease of hand-piecing. Michaeline has been sewing since she was 11 years old and has tried many kinds of needlecrafts. "I could never stick with them longer than a few months," says Michaeline. Several years ago, she noticed a quilt shop across the street from her bank, enrolled in a quiltmaking class, loved it, and now teaches quiltmaking. As Michaeline says, "I'm always thinking about quilts. I tend to be very experimental, and I enjoy all types of quilts."

Turn to our "Designer Gallery" and marvel at Michaeline's use of yukata (Japanese fabric) in her *Flights of Fancy* wall hanging.

Michaeline Reed
Pittsburgh, Pennsylvania

Compass Quest I
1983

"I just wanted to see if I could piece a Mariner's Compass," says Michaeline. "After I had successfully pieced the compass, I thought, why not use it in a quilt?" Michaeline then constructed the rest of the quilt in what she calls a "design-as-you-go" method. "At that time," confesses Michaeline, "I didn't have the slightest idea how else to do it. I just kept adding things until I decided to stop!"

Michaeline's oval compass was made from a pattern that she ordered through the mail. And the border design is from Jinny Beyer's border pattern book. (See "Resources" for information on both.)

Quilt Top Assembly

1. Join points (L, M) to the sides of point (H), as shown in Compass Piecing Diagram I. Join points (N, O) to the sides of point (I) in same fashion.

2. Join pieced arcs to sides of point (F), as shown in Compass Piecing Diagram II.

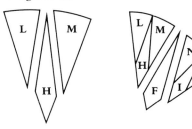

Compass Piecing Diagram I　　*Compass Piecing Diagram II*

3. Make another pieced arc, using points (P, J, Q, R, K, S, and G), as before. (See Compass Piecing Diagram III.) Join arcs to sides of point (E), as shown in Compass Piecing Diagram III. Make 2 pieced arcs, as shown, and 2 the mirror image of these. (See Compass Piecing Diagram V.)

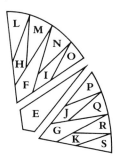

Compass Piecing Diagram III

4. Join 2 pieces (B) to the end of point (D), twice, as shown in Compass Piecing Diagram IV. Repeat using pieces C and A.

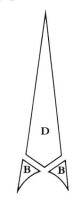

Compass Piecing Diagram IV

Compass Quest I

Finished Quilt Size
36″ x 42″

Fabric Requirements
Gold	— ½ yd.
Blue print	— 1 yd.
White/green print (WGP)	— 1¼ yd.
Paisley print	— 1 yd.
Maroon print	— ¼ yd.
Maroon	— 1½ yd.
Green★	— 1½ yd.
Backing	— 1½ yd.

★Includes yardage for binding.

Number to Cut
Template A	— 2 maroon
Template B	— 2 maroon print
Template B★	— 2 maroon print
Template C	— 2 maroon print
Template C★	— 2 maroon print
Template D	— 2 maroon
Template E	— 2 maroon
Template E★	— 2 maroon
Template F	— 2 green
Template F★	— 2 green
Template G	— 2 green
Template G★	— 2 green
Template H	— 2 WGP
Template H★	— 2 WGP
Template I	— 2 WGP
Template I★	— 2 WGP
Template J	— 2 WGP
Template J★	— 2 WGP
Template K	— 2 WGP
Template K★	— 2 WGP
Template L	— 2 gold
Template L★	— 2 gold
Template M	— 2 gold
Template M★	— 2 gold
Template N	— 2 gold
Template N★	— 2 gold
Template O	— 2 gold
Template O★	— 2 gold
Template P	— 2 gold
Template P★	— 2 gold
Template Q	— 2 gold
Template Q★	— 2 gold
Template R	— 2 gold
Template R★	— 2 gold
Template S	— 2 gold
Template S★	— 2 gold
Template T	— 1 paisley print
Template U	— 22 green
Template V	— 44 green
Template W	— 44 paisley print
Template X	— 26 green
Template X★	— 26 green
Template Y	— 26 WGP
Template Y★	— 26 WGP
Template Z	— 26 maroon print
Template Z★	— 26 maroon
Template AA	— 2 green
Template AA★	— 2 green
Template BB	— 2 green
Template BB★	— 2 green
Template CC	— 2 WGP
Template DD	— 2 WGP

★Flip or turn over template if fabric is one-sided.

5. Join arcs and points, as shown in Compass Piecing Diagram V, to complete oval. Appliqué piece (T) to center of oval.

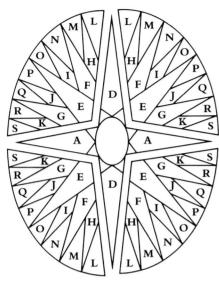

Compass Piecing Diagram V

6. Lay oval on blue print fabric. Measure 3½" from midpoints of oval's sides and 4" from midpoint of oval's top and bottom, as shown in Background Diagram. Add ¼" seam allowance to blue print background fabric and cut. Appliqué oval to background fabric. Cut out fabric from behind oval.

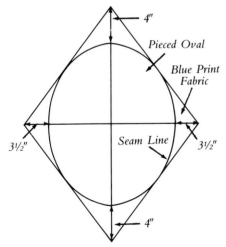

Background Diagram

7. Cut a rectangle, 20½" x 23¾", from maroon. Cut 4 border strips, 2½" wide, from paisley print. Join to maroon rectangle and miter corners. (See quilt photograph.)

8. Center oval on maroon rectangle and appliqué.

9. For flange on pieced borders, cut a 1"-wide strip from maroon and fold it in half lengthwise. Sew to long edges of triangles (AA and BB).

Join triangles (BB and CC), as shown in First Border Piecing Diagram, keeping folded edge of flange free of seam. Make 2 pieced borders and join to top and bottom of quilt.

Join triangles (AA and DD) in same manner and join to sides of quilt.

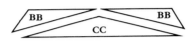

First Border Piecing Diagram

10. Cut 2 border strips, ¾" wide, from maroon and join to sides of quilt. Cut 2 border strips, ¾" wide, from maroon and join to top and bottom of quilt.

11. Join pieces (W, X, Y, and Z), as shown in Second Border Piecing Diagram I. (Refer to quilt photograph for color placement.) Make 22 sections, as shown, and 22, the mirror image of these, substituting maroon for the maroon print piece (Z). (See quilt photograph.) Join sections, as shown in Second Border Piecing Diagram II.

Join triangles (V) to the sides of square (U). Make 22 and join to complete border block, as shown in Second Border Piecing Diagram II.

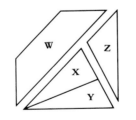

Second Border Piecing Diagram I

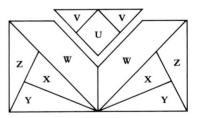

Second Border Piecing Diagram II

Join 6 border blocks at sides, twice, and join to sides of quilt.

Join 5 border blocks at sides, twice, and set aside.

12. Join triangles (X, Y, and Z), as shown in Corner Block Piecing Diagram, twice. Refer to quilt photograph for color placement. Make 4 corner blocks. Join corner blocks to each end of the two remaining borders. Join borders to top and bottom of quilt.

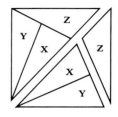

Corner Block Piecing Diagram

Quilting
Outline-quilt ¼" inside seam lines of all compass points. Michaeline quilted a shell in each corner of the maroon background and background-quilted the remaining area with radiating diagonal lines, 1" apart. A shell-and-rope pattern was quilted in triangles CC and DD. Outline-quilt ¼" inside seam line of triangles X, Y, and Z in the second border.

Finished Edges
Bind with green fabric.

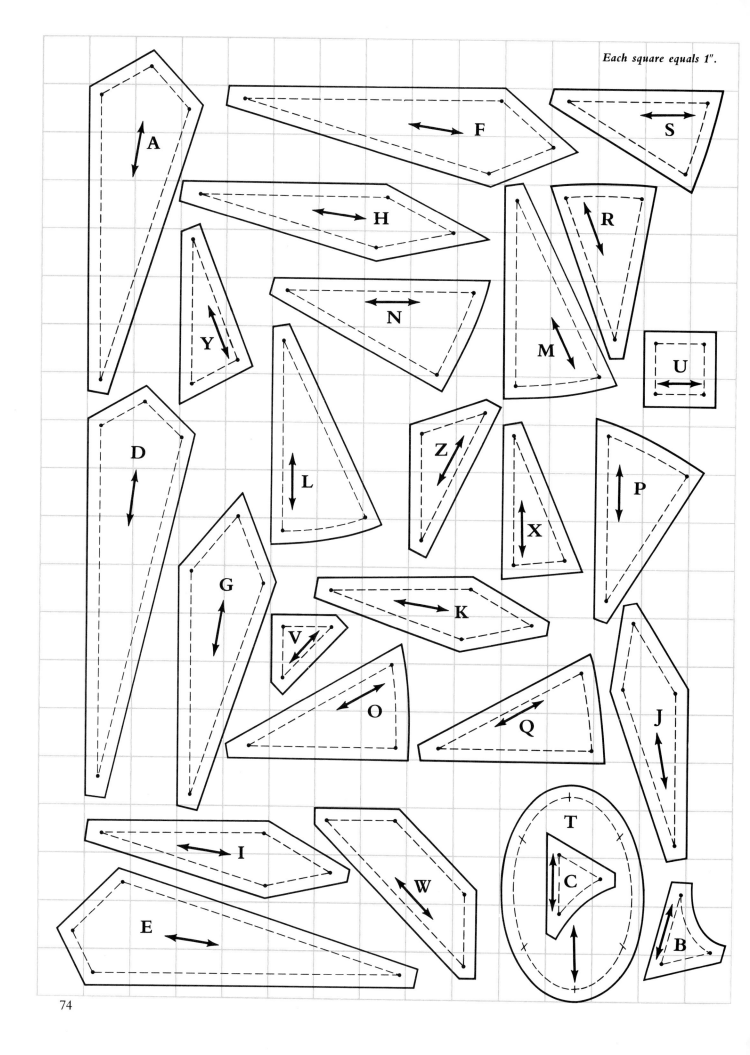

Each square equals 1".

74

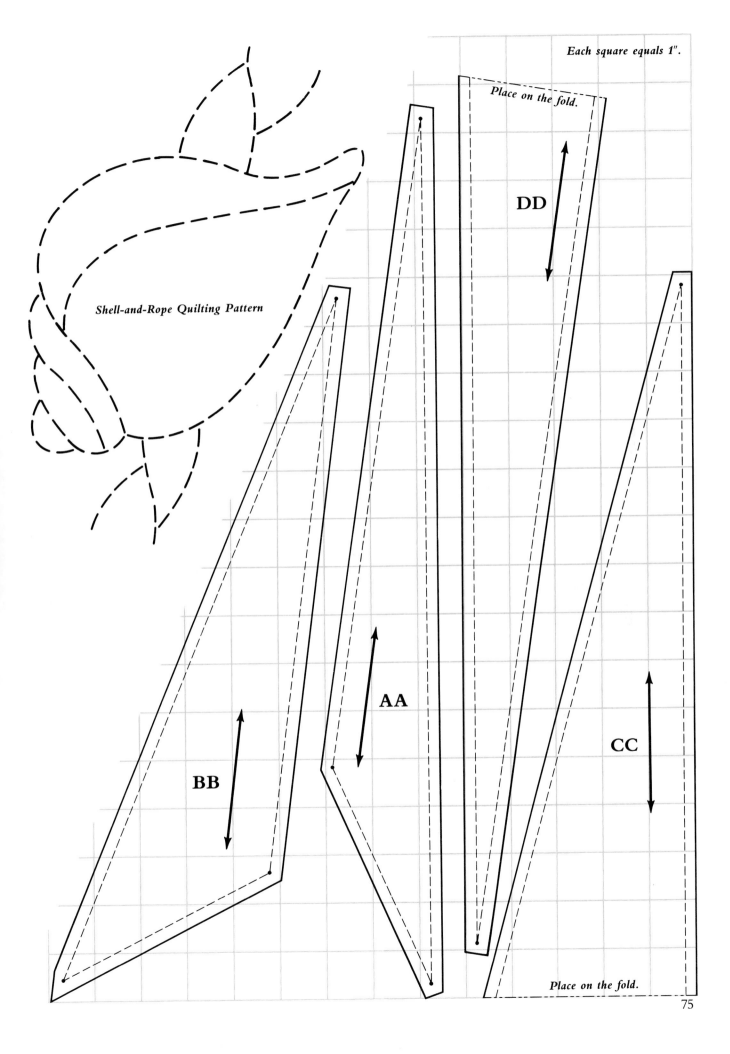

Each square equals 1".

Place on the fold.

DD

Shell-and-Rope Quilting Pattern

AA

BB

CC

Place on the fold.

75

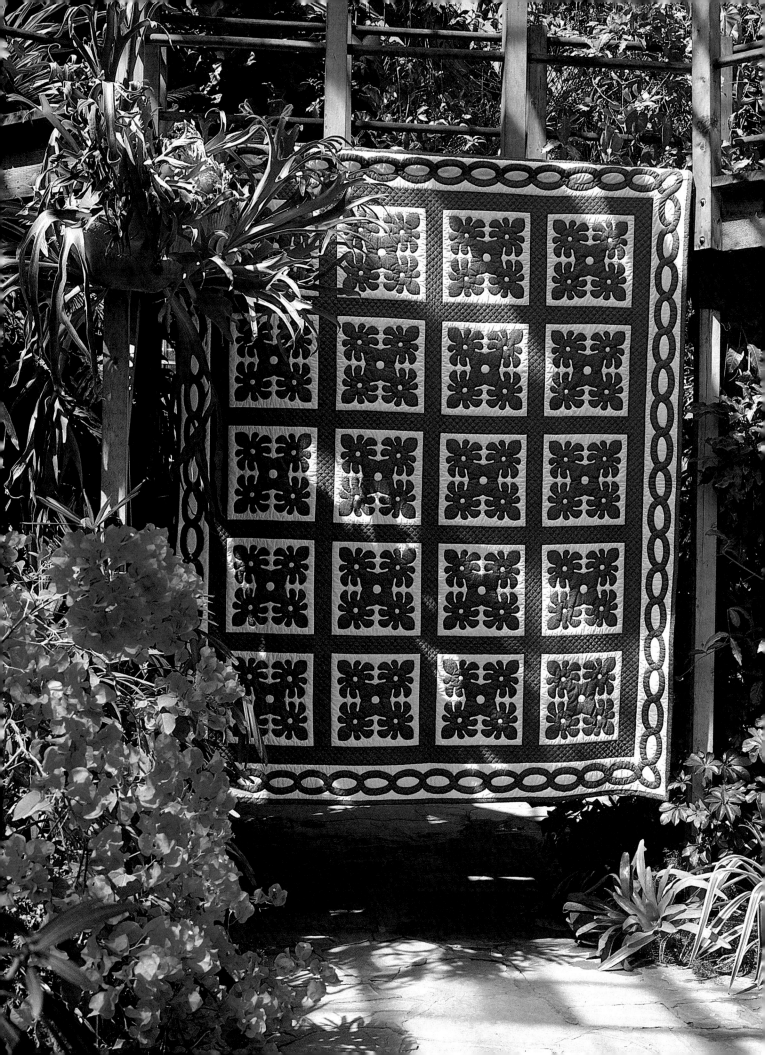

Pauline Spieks

Stone Mountain, Georgia

"I am a 'do it'!" proclaims Pauline. "I'm not a lecturer, but only a quilter who gets enthralled with my students and the classes that I teach. I love the fabrics, the people, and the patterns."

Quilting and her "doer" philosophy of life were the two ingredients that fueled Pauline's desire to become active again after a bout with a crippling and debilitating form of arthritis more than eight years ago. "I believe my arthritis was cured by my strong willpower to get to work on my quilts and to be creative again," recalls Pauline.

At 81, she teaches regularly at four different locations. Pauline tells us, "I stress superior workmanship in all phases of quiltmaking." Her favorite facet of quiltmaking is designing patchwork piecing for the best effect, efficiency, and minimal seams.

In our "Starmakers" chapter we feature Pauline's *Star and Crescent* quilt, the quilt she made after completing *Williamsburg Palm*.

Williamsburg Palm
1983

Pauline's *Williamsburg Palm* is made using Hawaiian and freezer paper appliqué techniques. Its design is very similar to a quilt, made in 1861, by a lady named Mary Grove; and that is why it is sometimes known as the Blue Grove quilt pattern. (See "Resources.")

In the quilt made by Mary Grove, yards of bias strips were used to form the cable border. But Pauline and her good friend Ann Oliver put their heads together and devised an easier and more accurate method for appliquéing the cable border, using pattern pieces instead of long bias strips. Their ingenuity was recognized in a national quilt magazine a few years ago. (See "Resources.")

The blue reminded Pauline of a Williamsburg blue, and the appliqué shape reminded her of a palm leaf—thus, the name *Williamsburg Palm*.

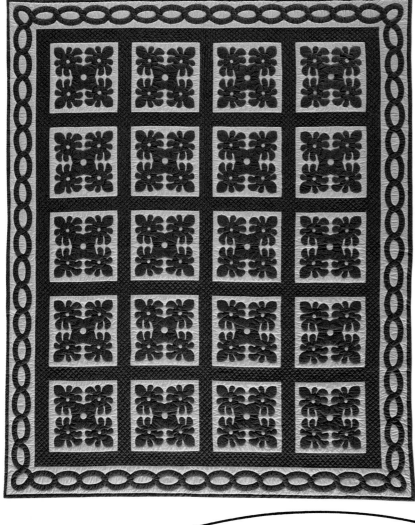

Williamsburg Palm

Finished Quilt Size
87″ x 105″

**Number of Blocks and
Finished Size**
20 blocks—15″ x 15″

Fabric Requirements
Blue print   —11¼ yd.
Muslin   —6½ yd.
Blue print for
  bias binding   —1¼ yd.
Backing   —9 yd.

Other Materials
Freezer paper

Number to Cut
Template A   —58 blue print
Template B   —4 blue print
Template C   —4 blue print

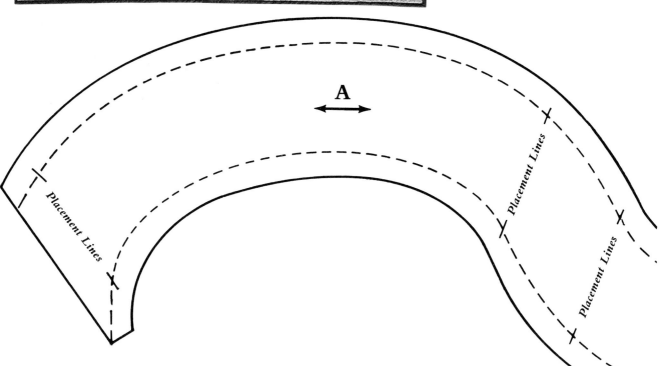

Quilt Top Assembly

1. Cut twenty 15½" squares from muslin and set aside.

2. Cut twenty 19" squares from blue print. Fold blue print squares in half twice. Lay palm leaf template on folded fabric. (See Palm Leaf Placement Diagram.) Cut along curved edges, as shown. Unfold fabric and set aside. Cut 20 palm leaves.

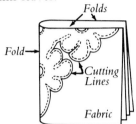

Palm Leaf Placement Diagram

3. Trace the complete palm leaf pattern *without seam allowances* on the dull side of a 19" square of freezer paper. Cut out pattern. Make 20.

Center the freezer-paper pattern, with shiny side up, on the wrong side of the fabric palm leaf and pin in place. Turn seam allowance under, clipping where needed to smooth curves, and press to shiny side of freezer paper to fuse fabric to paper.

Center palm leaf on muslin square and appliqué. Appliqué 20 blocks. Cut muslin from behind the appliquéd palm leaf and gently remove freezer paper.

4. Cut 16 sashing strips, 3½" wide, from blue print. Alternate 5 blocks with 4 sashing strips to form a vertical row, as shown in Setting Diagram. Make 4 vertical rows.

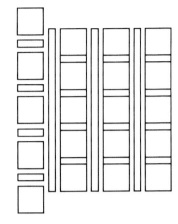

Setting Diagram

5. Cut 3 sashing strips, 3½" wide, from blue print. Alternate 4 vertical rows with 3 sashing strips, as shown in Setting Diagram, and join.

6. Cut 4 borders, 3½" wide, from blue print. Join to quilt and miter corners.

7. Cut 4 borders, 6½" wide, from muslin. Before appliquéing cable to border, lightly mark a line down the center of each border, lengthwise. This will be your cable placement line. Prepare cable pieces (A, B, and C) using freezer paper, as directed in step 3.

Refer to the Cable Placement

Diagram and pin pieces to border. Note the over-and-under placement so that no seam lines are showing. Appliqué cable, except for corner pieces, which will be appliquéd after borders are joined to the quilt. Cut muslin from behind each cable piece and remove freezer paper.

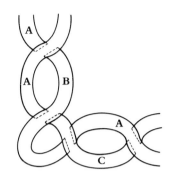

Cable Placement Diagram

8. Join appliquéd borders to quilt and miter corners. Appliqué corner pieces. Remove freezer paper.

Quilting

Pauline outline-quilted outside all appliquéd edges. Diagonal ¾" cross-hatching was quilted on all sashing strips.

Finished Edges

Bind with blue print fabric.

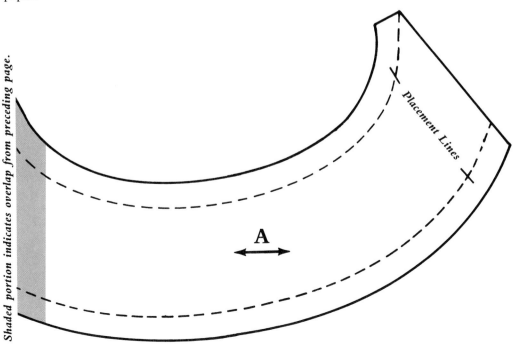

Shaded portion indicates overlap from preceding page.

A

Placement Lines

79

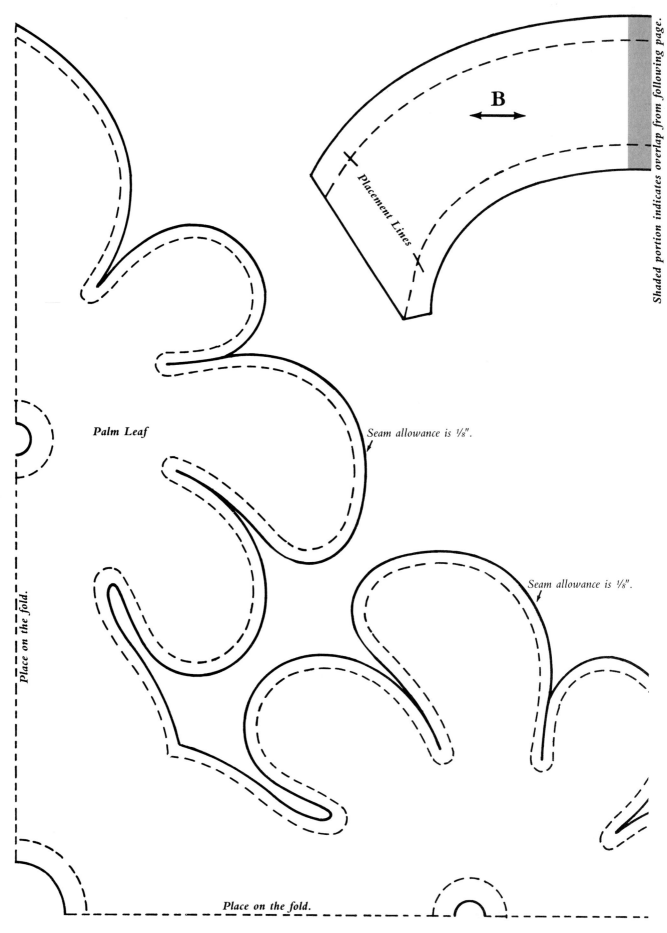

Shaded portion indicates overlap from following page.

B

Placement Lines

Palm Leaf

Seam allowance is ⅛".

Seam allowance is ⅛".

Place on the fold.

Place on the fold.

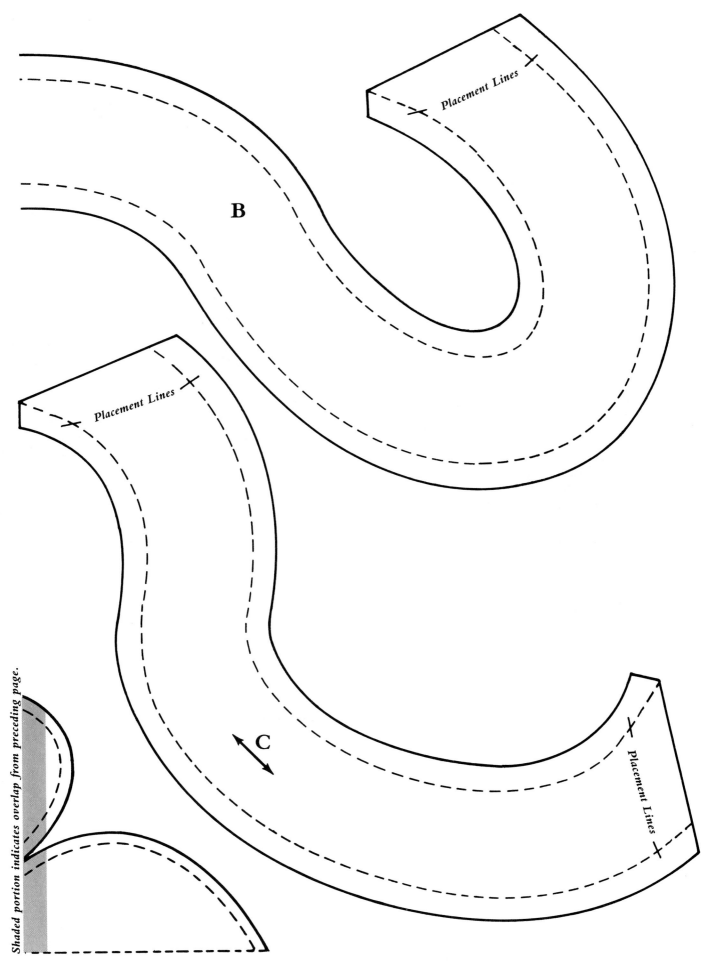

B

Placement Lines

Placement Lines

C

Placement Lines

81

Susan Denise Brucker

Lanexa, Virginia

The first time Susan attended a quiltmaking class, she knew she was hooked. "The joyous anticipation, warm fellowship, and piles of fabrics that were begging to be cut and pieced into something wonderful were enough to get me hooked on quilting for a long time," says Susan. When she was ten, Susan began sewing by making clothes for her doll from scraps her grandmother gave her. Sixteen years later, she combined her sewing talent with her love for color and fabric designs to make her first quilt.

With quiltmaking, Susan enjoys a sense of accomplishment that comes with each step. "I am a very task-oriented person," says Susan. "So with quilting, it is easy to say, I have finished choosing the fabric; I have finished cutting it out; I have finished piecing; I have put it on the frame; the quilting is done; and the binding is attached."

Susan is a member of the James River Heritage Chapter of the Richmond Quilter's Guild, Richmond, Virginia, and the statewide quilting organization, Virginia Consortium of Quilters.

Basket Full of Memories
1987

"This one is for me!" exclaims Susan. All of Susan's previous quilts (nine, to be exact) have gone to family and friends. While anticipating the joy of quilting for herself, she was surprised to discover that it was quite difficult to select the fabric and pattern that were truly her favorites for this special quilt. Midway through her search, she remembered the many beautiful fabrics she had already used in making her quilts. "So I gathered all my scraps from those quilts and selected a pattern that could utilize all of those fabrics," says Susan. Once these decisions were out of the way, Susan recalls, "This quilt provided me with loads of memories of the hours I had worked on other quilts and of the people and occasions that had inspired them."

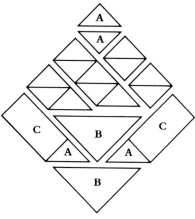

Diagram. Make 2. Join to sides of pieced square. Join beige print triangle (B) to complete block. Make 32 blocks.

Basket Block Piecing Diagram

2. Join white print triangles (D) to dark brown print I triangles (D) to make 31 pieced-accent squares.
3. Join lattice strips (I) to sides of blocks to form a block row, as shown in Setting Diagram.

Setting Diagram

Basket Full of Memories

Finished Quilt Size
72″ x 87″

Number of Blocks and Finished Size
32 blocks—9″ x 9″

Fabric Requirements
Beige prints — 2½ yd. total
Dk. brown print I — 2⅛ yd.
Dk. brown print II — 2½ yd.
White print — 2½ yd.
Tan print — 1⅝ yd.
Scraps — 1¼ yd. total
Dk. brown print II
  for bias binding — 1 yd.
Backing — 5 yd.

Number to Cut
Template A — 308 beige prints
  80 dk. brown print I
  64 dk. brown print II
  84 white print
  40 tan print
  272 scraps

Template B — 32 beige prints
  32 dk. brown print I
Template C — 64 beige prints
Template D — 49 dk. brown print I
  31 white print
Template E — 14 dk. brown print I
Template E★ — 14 dk. brown print I
Template F — 4 dk. brown print II
Template G — 14 white print
Template H — 4 tan print
Template I — 80 tan print
★Flip or turn over template if fabric is one-sided.

Quilt Top Assembly
1. Join 6 scrap triangles (A) with 8 beige print triangles (A) in three rows, as shown in Basket Block Piecing Diagram. Join rows. Join to dark brown print I triangle (B) to form a pieced square.

Join a dark brown print II triangle (A) to the end of rectangle (C), as shown in Basket Block Piecing

4. Join 2 triangles (E) to the sides of triangle (G) to make pieced-triangle inset. (See Setting Diagram.) Make 14. Join to ends of block rows, as shown in Setting Diagram.
5. Join triangles (F) to ends of 2 block rows, as shown.

6. Join lattice strips (I) to remaining dark brown print triangles (D) and pieced-accent squares to form a lattice strip row, as shown in Setting Diagram.

7. Join block rows and lattice strip rows. Join triangles (F) to quilt corners, as shown.

8. Cut 2 borders, 2″ wide, from white print and join to top and bottom of quilt.

9. Cut 2 borders, 2″ wide, from white print and join to sides of quilt.

10. Alternate 19 white print triangles (A) with 18 scrap triangles (A) and join at sides to make first pieced border. Make a pieced border each for top and bottom of quilt. Note that Susan put her scrap triangles in the same order for each strip. (See quilt photograph.)

11. Alternate 18 dark brown print I triangles (A) with 5 tan print triangles (A) and 12 beige print triangles (A) and join in the same fashion as above to make second pieced border. Susan alternated one tan print triangle with two beige print triangles. (See quilt photograph.) Make 2 pieced borders.

Join first pieced border to second pieced border, twice, with scrap triangles and dark brown print I triangles at seam line. (See quilt photograph.) Join borders to the top and bottom of quilt with white print triangles at seam line.

12. Alternate 23 white print triangles (A) with 22 scrap triangles (A) and join in same fashion as in step 10 to make first pieced border for side of quilt. Make 2 and set aside. Borders will be slightly shorter than sides of quilt.

13. Alternate 22 dark brown print I triangles (A) with 7 tan print triangles (A) and 14 beige print triangles (A) for second pieced border. Join in the same fashion as in step 10. Put tan and beige print triangles in the same order as in step 11. Make 2. Borders will be slightly shorter than sides of quilt.

14. Join first pieced border to second pieced border as in step 11.

Begin at the top edge of quilt side and *place* borders along sides with the white print triangles next to quilt edge. Measure the distance from point 1 to point 2, as shown in Pieced Border Diagram. Cut a piece of white print fabric to adjust the length of each side border and

join to borders. Join borders to sides of quilt.

15. Join 4 tan print triangles (A) with square (H), as shown in Corner Piecing Diagram. Make 4 pieced corners and join to quilt.

16. Cut 2 borders, 2″ wide, from dark brown print II and join to sides of quilt.

17. Cut 2 borders, 2″ wide, from dark brown print II and join to top and bottom of quilt.

Quilting

Susan outline-quilted ¼″ inside seam line of all pieces of the basket blocks and of all triangles in the pieced borders.

Finished Edges

Bind with dark brown print II.

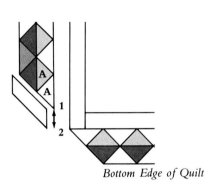

Bottom Edge of Quilt

Pieced Border Diagram

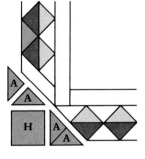

Corner Piecing Diagram

☐ *white print* ▨ *tan print*
☐ *scraps* ■ *dk. brown print I*

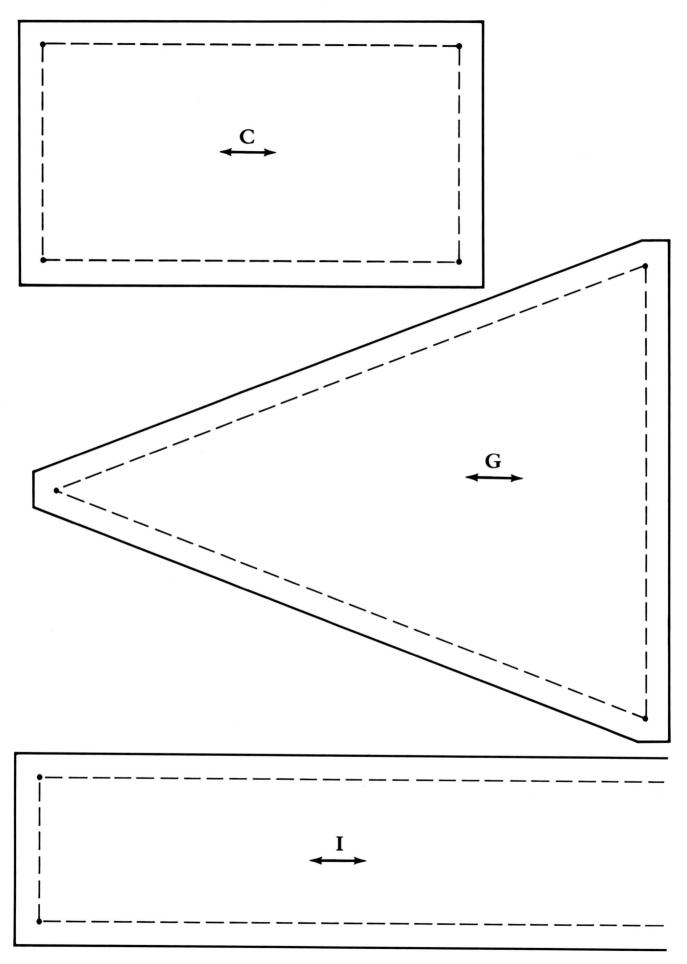

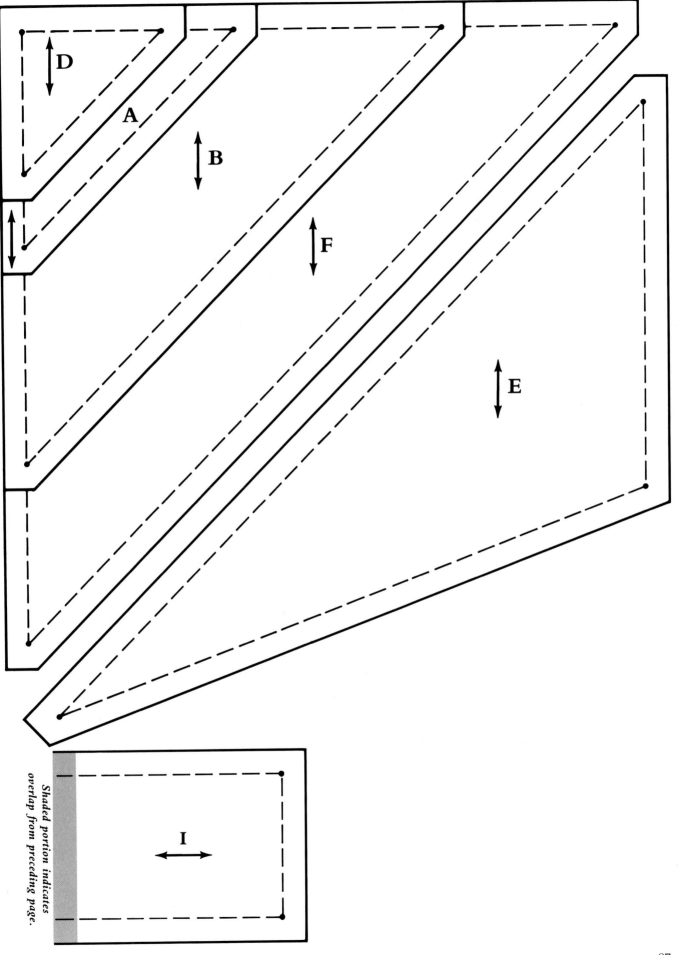

A

D

B

F

E

I

Shaded portion indicates overlap from preceding page.

87

Ann M. Hargis
Pullman, Washington

Ann was new to the Pullman area and searching for a respite from the scientific world of veterinary medicine, when a friend encouraged her to try quilting. Since Ann didn't sew, she was rather hesitant, and as her friend, Susan Brucker (see page 82), told us, "I almost had to drag her to her first quilting class." As quilting often does, it quickly won Ann's heart. "It has brought another perspective to my life," says Ann. "I have made new women friends, have learned much about my heritage, and have been able to fulfill a creative need in my life."

Migration Quilt
1983

The changes in nature that occur because of the Earth's orbit are expressed throughout Ann's quilt. The title, the interlocking patchwork, the quilting, and the colors all characterize the essence of the seasons. Quilted in the center of the octagons are birds—half of them facing one direction (flying north) and the other half facing in the opposite direction (flying south). The colors—blues and greens for winter, reds and oranges for summer, and the tones in between for spring and fall—portray a seasonal panorama that makes us realize how the Earth is in a constant state of transition.

As a veterinarian, Ann was especially inspired to make a quilt that symbolized her love for animals and nature. "Just as the rings in *Migration*'s patchwork interlock," Ann explains, "I feel my life is interlocked with animals and nature."

Migration won a blue ribbon and first place in the Contemporary Quilt Division of the Palouse Empire Fair in Colfax, Washington, in 1983.

Migration Quilt

Finished Quilt Size
72½" x 87½"

Fabric Requirements
Black	—4 yd.
4 or 5 shades of 11 colors	—¼ yd. each
Black for bias binding	—1 yd.
Backing	—6 yd.

Number to Cut
Template A	—50 black
Template B	—84 black 196 total★
Template C	—52 black 99 total★
Template D	—22 black 165 total★

★See colored drawing of quilt and quilt photograph. As a guideline, the *majority* of the quilt requires 4 of each color for B, 2 of each color for C, and 3 of each color for D. Arranging pieces as you cut them, as described in step 1, is recommended by Ann.

Quilt Top Assembly
1. Refer to colored drawing of quilt and quilt photograph. Arrange all pieces on a large work surface before joining. Ann says that, because pieces are easy to sew together incorrectly, you should choose a work area that will not be disturbed. If no such area is available, she suggests placing each row of pieces in a numbered bag.
2. Join pieces for blocks 1, 2, 3, and 4, as shown in Block Piecing Diagrams.
3. Join blocks at sides to form rows, as shown in Setting Diagram. Join rows.
4. Join pieces to form top and bottom strips and join to quilt.

Quilting
Outline-quilt ¼" from seam lines of each ring. Outline-quilt ½" from seam line of each octagon (A). Quilt a bird inside each octagon. Quilt a heart inside each center square (C) of block 3.

Finished Edges
Bind with black fabric.

Block 1

Block 2

Block 3

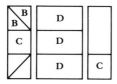

Block 4

Block Piecing Diagrams

Top Strip

Bottom Strip

Setting Diagram

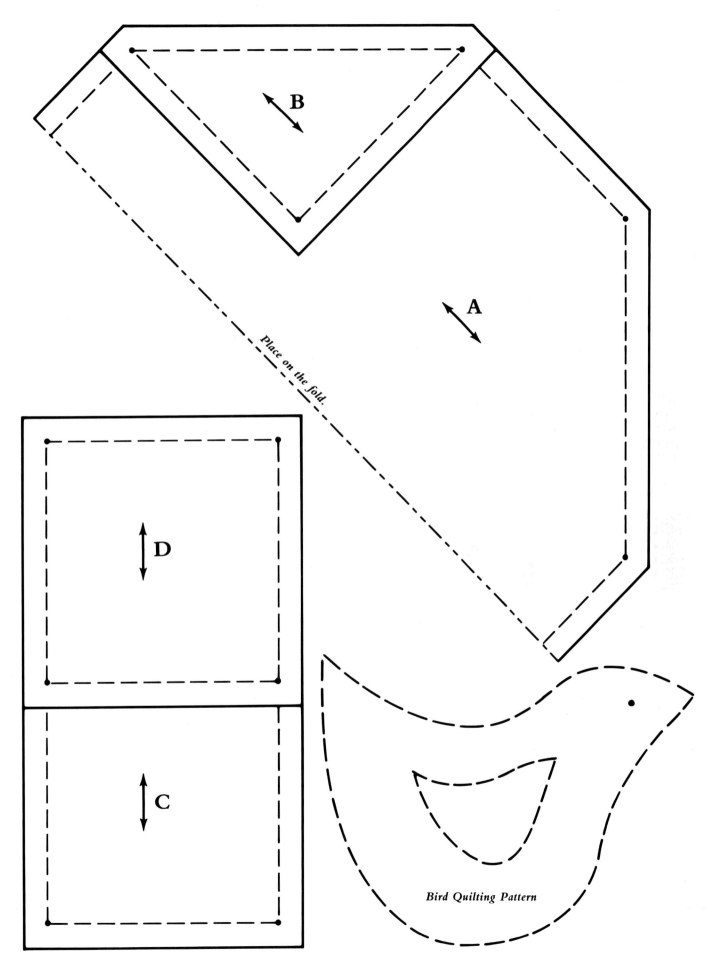

B

A

Place on the fold.

D

C

Bird Quilting Pattern

91

Donna Lake
Noti, Oregon

"Friends to care and share" are treasured benefits of quiltmaking for Donna. "Three words come to mind when I think of quilts—love, friendship, and contentment," says Donna. Quilting once a week with several friends has provided the encouragement that has contributed to the excellence of Donna's quilting today.

Quiltmaking has also given her the pride and self-esteem that women often seek after the children leave home. "When someone asks if I work," says Donna, "I stand up proudly and say, 'Yes, I'm a quiltmaker.'"

Donna's quilt, *Starry Castle*, graces our cover. You'll find instructions for it in our "Starmakers" chapter.

Ribbons 'n Rings
1988

It seems that *Ribbons 'n Rings* is a more than appropriate name for Donna's quilt, since it has had a cluster of blue ribbons pinned to its surface in its short life span. It won First Place in Patchwork at the Lane Country Fair and first place at the State and National Grange, both in Oregon in 1988.

The idea for *Ribbons 'n Rings* began while Donna was playing with a protractor—"and this design just happened," says Donna. If you plan to make Donna's quilt, pay close attention to your template placement on the fabric before cutting. Donna centered a flower in each triangle before cutting, which makes this quilt extra-special.

Though Donna is truly thrilled by the accolades her quilts receive, she says, "More importantly, you meet some of the nicest people. That I will always treasure."

Ribbons n' Rings

Finished Quilt Size
105″ x 105″

Number of Blocks and Finished Size
9 blocks—24″ x 24″

Fabric Requirements
Blue paisley —¾ yd.
Blue print —3¾ yd.
Maroon print —1⅞ yd.
Blue/maroon stripe —3¼ yd.
Purple print —2⅝ yd.
Pink print —6¼ yd.
Blue print for
bias binding★ —2½ yd.
Backing —9 yd.
★Includes yardage for bias strips appliquéd to quilt.

Number to Cut
Template A —72 blue paisley
Template B —36 blue print
Template B★★ —36 blue print
Template C —72 maroon print
Template C★★—72 maroon print
Template D —360 blue print
288 maroon print
Template E —36 blue/maroon
stripe
Template F —180 purple print
Template G —144 blue print
Template H —36 pink print
Template I —36 pink print
Template J —192 blue print
196 purple print
Template K —4 blue print
★★Flip or turn over template if fabric is one-sided.

Quilt Top Assembly
1. Join 8 pieces (A) to form a circle, as shown in Block Piecing Diagram I.

Block Piecing Diagram I

2. Alternate blue print and maroon print triangles (B, C, D) to form a strip, as shown in Block Piecing Diagram II and quilt block photograph. Make 8 strips, half of them mirror images of the others.

Join strips to opposite sides of piece (E), as shown. Make 4 sets. Join 2 sets to the opposite sides of pieced circle, as shown.

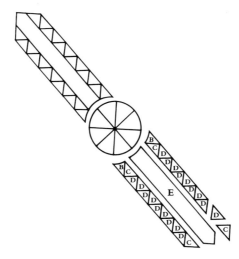

Block Piecing Diagram II

3. Alternate 4 triangles (G) with 5 triangles (F) to form an arc, as shown in Block Piecing Diagram III. Join pieces (H, I) to opposite sides of arc to form a pieced triangle, as shown. Make 4 pieced triangles. Join to opposite sides of remaining sets made in step 2. Join to center piece to complete block, as shown. Make 9 blocks.

Block Piecing Diagram III

4. Join blocks at sides to form 3 rows of 3 blocks each. Join rows.
5. Cut 4 borders, 2¼″ wide, from blue/maroon stripe. (See quilt photograph.) Join to quilt and miter corners.
6. Cut 4 borders, 10″ wide, from pink print. Join to quilt and miter corners.

Appliqué 1″-wide (includes seam allowance) bias strip from blue print in arc pattern, as shown in quilt photograph.
7. Cut 4 borders, 1¼″ wide, from blue/maroon stripe. Join to quilt and miter corners.
8. Alternate 48 blue print triangles (J) with 49 purple print triangles (J) and join at sides to form pieced border. Make 4.

Join 2 borders to opposite sides of quilt. Join corner pieces (K) to ends of remaining 2 borders. Join borders to quilt.
9. Cut 4 borders, 2″ wide, from blue/maroon stripe. Join to quilt and miter corners.

Quilting
Donna emphasized the circular patchwork pattern by repeated lines of circular quilting, ½″ apart. (See quilt photograph.) Feathers were quilted along pink print borders with diagonal lines of background quilting, 1″ apart. Triangles in pieced borders are outline-quilted, ¼″ inside seam lines.

Finished Edges
Bind with blue print fabric.

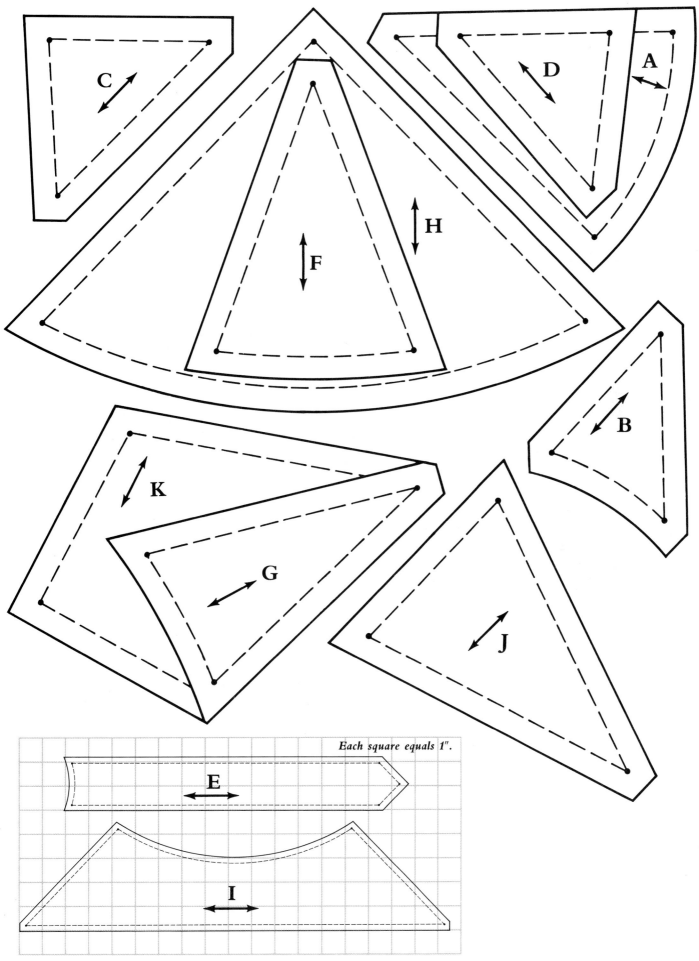

Each square equals 1".

95

Hope Shoaf
Little Rock, Arkansas

"Nothing in my fascinating life has affected me more than quilting," said Hope. As a young photographer in New York City, Hope found that often people asked her more questions about her hobby, quilting, than they did about photography. "At that time," said Hope, "quilting was almost a lost art. Suddenly I was in demand to speak to ladies' clubs and groups about quilting." Hope continued, "I had no slides, so I would make an exhibit of my quilts, wear a dress with trapunto accents, and talk about the history of quilting." Sometime later, an article about Hope and her quilting was published in *The New York Times*.

In 1974, after moving to a 40-acre farm in her native Arkansas, Hope continued to quilt and to lecture wherever she was invited. She was especially proud of the Christmas quilts she designed to be auctioned off each year to finance cancer treatments for the poor.

While we were composing Hope's story for our book, Hope died after a long illness. During her last months she talked about slowing down just a little, but her enthusiasm for quilting never waned. She remarked, "I still have to keep my hands busy. I can't stay away from quilting."

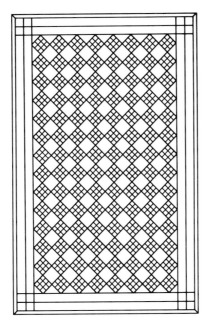

Hope's Double Nine Patch
1974
Strip-pieced and small in size, *Hope's Double Nine Patch* is just what's needed for a quick quilting pick-me-up. Set on the diagonal, this Double Nine Patch is a beginner's delight.

Hope's Double Nine Patch

Finished Quilt Size
46″ x 76″

Number of Blocks and Finished Size
112 blocks—3⅜″ x 3⅜″

Fabric Requirements
Orange	—2⅛ yd.
Muslin	—3½ yd.
Orange for bias binding	—1 yd.
Backing	—4½ yd.

Number to Cut
Template A★	—560 orange	
	448 muslin	
Template B	—8 orange	
	8 muslin	
Template C	—91 muslin	
Template D	—40 muslin	
Template E	—4 muslin	

★If you prefer to use strip-piecing, see step 1 and do not use template A.

Quilt Top Assembly
1. Alternate colors and join squares (A) at sides to form 3 rows, as shown in Block Piecing Diagram. Join rows to complete block. Make 112 blocks.

Block Piecing Diagram

If you are strip-piecing, cut cross-grained strips, 1⅝″ wide, from orange and muslin fabrics. Join 3 strips together, alternating colors, to make a set. Make 2 kinds of sets: orange-muslin-orange and muslin-orange-muslin. Cut across strips at 1⅝″ intervals. Join as shown in Block Piecing Diagram. Make 112 blocks.

2. Alternate blocks with squares (C) and triangles (D, E) to form rows, as shown in Setting Diagram I. Join rows.

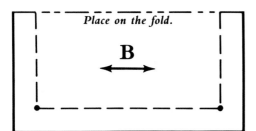

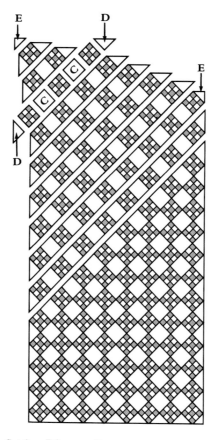

Setting Diagram I

3. Cut 4 borders, 2½″ wide, from orange and 4 from muslin, as shown in Setting Diagram II. (See whole quilt drawing.) Join muslin borders to orange borders, as shown. Join borders to top and bottom of quilt.

Make 4 four-patch squares, as shown, and join to the ends of the remaining borders. Join to quilt.

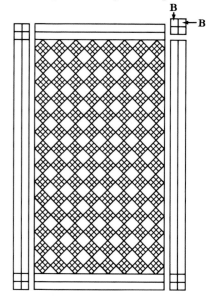

Setting Diagram II

Quilting
Outline-quilt outside seam line of all squares and borders. Hope quilted a circle in the center of each muslin square.

Finished Edges
Bind with orange fabric.

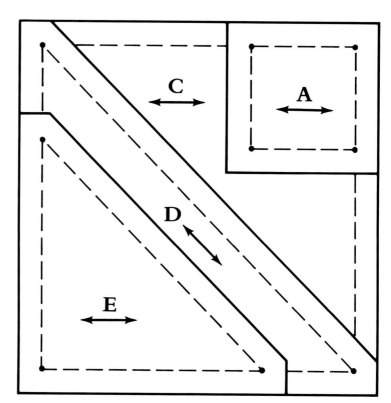

This avid golfer, swimmer, former professional interior designer, needlepointer, and knitter has been enamored of quilting for the last three years. "I have so many quilt designs in my head that I will have to live to 2087 to complete them all!" exclaims Tommi.

Tommi is a self-taught quilter and prefers the traditional patterns, spiced with her own interpretation, although she does enjoy creating some of her own patterns. Inspiration for her original designs comes from nature and architecture. "Quilting fulfills my need to be creative and my desire to remain at home with my retired husband," says Tommi. "And, as with everything else in my life, I have much support and encouragement from my husband, daughters, and grandchildren."

Tommi Marten
Spring Mills, Pennsylvania

Tommi's Castle Wall
1986
This stunning bed-size quilt of blue-gray and burgundy prints and stripes is Tommi's interpretation of the traditional pattern, Castle Wall.

"Playing around with the striped fabric, I found I could make a kaleidoscope design by cutting it in various directions," says Tommi. "It was all great fun."

In 1987, *Tommi's Castle Wall* won first prize at the Centre County Grange Fair, Centre Hall, Pennsylvania, and Best of Show at the Big Valley Octoberfest, Easton, Pennsylvania.

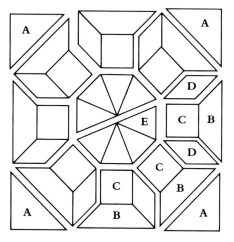

Block Piecing Diagram

Tommi's Castle Wall

Finished Quilt Size
94" x 105"

Number of Blocks and Finished Size
30 Castle Wall blocks—11" x 11"

Fabric Requirements

Burgundy flower vine print	—1 yd.
Stripe print I	—2 yd.
Stripe print II	—3 yd.
Burgundy print	—¾ yd.
Med. blue floral print	—¾ yd.
Navy print	—4 yd.
Gray floral print	—1½ yd.
Navy	—2¼ yd.
Bias binding (optional)	—1 yd.
Backing	—9 yd.

Number to Cut

Template A	—120 burgundy flower vine print
Template B	—240 stripe print I
Template C	—120 burgundy print
	120 med. blue floral print
Template D	—240 navy print
Template E★	—240 gray floral print

★Using the two-mirror technique may be helpful with template placement. (See Editor's Note, page 6.)

Quilt Top Assembly
1. Join 8 triangles (E) at sides, as shown in Block Piecing Diagram. Join squares (C), diamonds (D), and trapezoids (B) to center piece. (Alternate burgundy print and med. blue floral print squares (C) when joining.)

Complete block by joining triangles (A) to sides of trapezoids (B), as shown in Block Piecing Diagram. Make 30 blocks.
2. Join blocks at sides in 5 rows of 6 blocks each. (See quilt photograph.) Join rows.
3. Cut 4 borders, 3" wide, from navy. Join to quilt and miter corners.
4. Cut 4 borders, 3¾" wide, from stripe print II. Join to quilt and miter corners.
5. Cut 4 borders, 10¾" wide, from navy print. Join to quilt and miter corners.
6. Cut 4 borders, 3¾" wide, from stripe print II. Join to quilt and miter corners.

Quilting
Tommi quilted in-the-ditch of all block pieces, and hearts were quilted on triangles (A). A rope pattern was quilted on the navy border strips, and she followed the floral design on the border prints. Parallel lines, 1" apart, were quilted on the navy print border.

Finished Edges
Tommi preferred to finish the edges without a binding. To use this method, trim quilt batting to the seam line, and the quilt top and backing to the seam allowance. Turn seam allowances to the inside and blindstitch together.

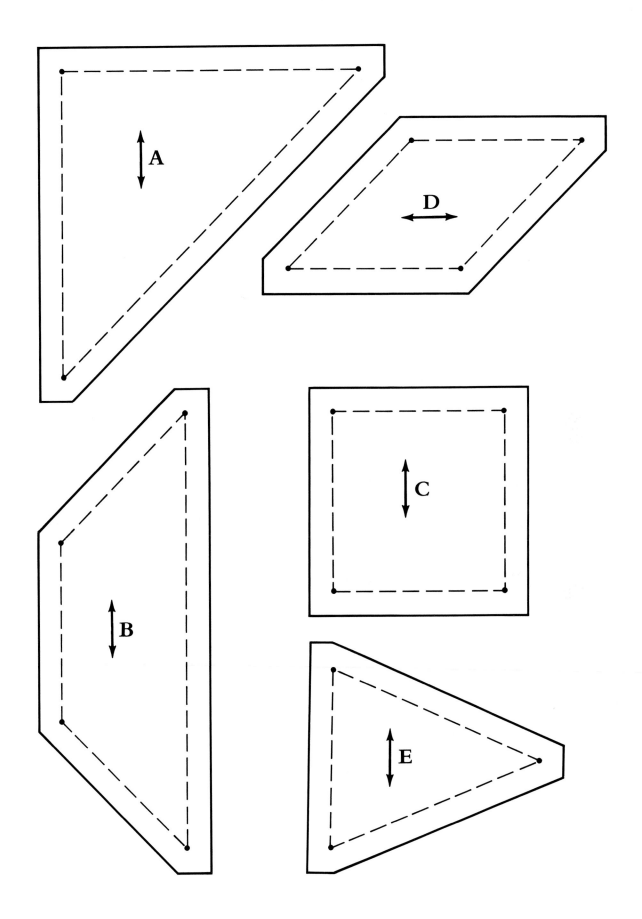

Patricia Eaton

McRae, Arkansas

Teaching a quilting class is something Patricia thought she would never have the nerve to do. "But quilting has given me the confidence to do things, such as teaching, that I probably would never have tried before," says Patricia. "I can create things that give a certain amount of pleasure to others, and in turn I get a lot of pleasure from it."

Patricia has been quilting for the past nine years, and all her quilts are hand-pieced and hand-quilted. According to Patricia, her quilting activities have turned her husband and son into self-appointed quilt critics and advice givers. Says Patricia, "It really makes home life interesting sometimes!"

Bear's Paw
1982

This quilt is very special to Patricia for two reasons. First, it was her first pieced quilt, and second, it was the only survivor of a fire that burned the local quilt shop to the ground in 1986. "We thought the quilt was a goner," recalls Patricia. "But evidently the firemen had sprayed so much water on the building that the quilt was too wet to burn." *Bear's Paw* was found intact among a heap of ashes and charred timbers. "It was totally black and covered with roofing material and soot," says Patricia. "I feel very fortunate to still have the quilt, and I especially enjoy showing it." *Bear's Paw* won first place in the hand-pieced, hand-quilted category at the 1982 Harrison Quilt Show, Harrison, Arkansas, and Grand Prize at the Searcy Quilt Show, Searcy, Arkansas, in 1982.

Bear's Paw

Finished Quilt Size
88″ x 106″

Number of Blocks and Finished Size
20 Bear's Paw
blocks—15¾″ x 15¾″

Fabric Requirements
Blue print — 4 yd.
White — 6¼ yd.
Blue print for
bias binding — 1 yd.
Backing — 9 yd.

Number to Cut
Template A — 80 blue print
Template B★ — 488 blue print
488 white
Template C — 50 blue print
80 white
Template D — 80 white
★Rather than cutting individual triangles, some quilters may prefer the quick machine-piecing method for pieced squares. See step 9.

Quilt Top Assembly
1. Join 4 blue print triangles (B) to 4 white triangles (B) to form pieced squares, as shown in Section Piecing Diagram. (If using the quick machine-piecing method for pieced squares, pieced squares are ready for joining.) Join pieced squares to form strips, as shown, and join a white square (C) to the end of one strip. Join short strip to side of blue print square (A) first. Join remaining strip to the adjacent side of square (A), as shown. Make 80 sections.

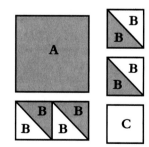

Section Piecing Diagram

2. Alternate 2 sections with white rectangle (D) and join at sides to form a unit, as shown in Block Piecing Diagram. Make 2. Join 2

white rectangles (D) to opposite sides of blue print square (C), as shown. Alternate units and pieced strip, as shown, and join to complete block. Make 20 blocks.

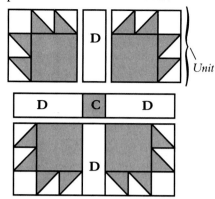

Block Piecing Diagram

3. Cut 25 sashing strips, 2¾″ wide, from white. Refer to whole quilt drawing and alternate 5 sashing strips with 4 blocks, beginning and ending with a sashing strip. Join strips and blocks at sides to form a row. Make 5 block rows.
   Cut 24 sashing strips, 2¾″ wide, from white. Alternate 5 blue print accent squares (C) with 4 sashing strips. (See quilt drawing.) Join squares and strips at sides to form a sashing row. Make 6 rows.
4. Alternate sashing rows with block rows, beginning and ending with a sashing row, and join.
5. Cut 2 border strips, 2¾″ wide, from blue print. Join to the top and bottom of quilt.
6. Cut 2 border strips, 2¾″ wide, from blue print. Join to the sides of quilt.
7. Cut 2 border strips, 2¾″ wide, from white. Join to top and bottom of quilt.
8. Cut 2 border strips, 2¾″ wide, from white. Join to the sides of quilt.
9. Make a sawtooth border with 168 pieced squares made with blue print triangles (B) and white triangles (B). For the quick machine-piecing method for pieced squares, lay two fabric rectangles (one white and one blue print) of equal size, right sides together, with the blue print rectangle on the bottom. Mark a grid of 3⅛″ squares on the top fabric. Draw a diagonal line through each square. Machine-stitch

¼″ on either side of diagonal lines. (See Pieced Squares Diagram.) Cut along marked lines.

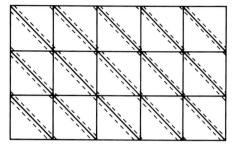

Pieced Squares Diagram

Join 37 pieced squares at sides to form a border strip. (See quilt drawing for proper placement.) Make 2 border strips. Join strips to top and bottom of quilt.
   Join 47 pieced squares at sides for side border strip. (This number includes the corner squares. Be sure to refer to quilt drawing for proper placement of corner squares.) Make 2 border strips. Join to the sides of quilt.

Quilting
Outline-quilt ¼″ inside seam lines, as shown in Quilting Diagram. Parallel quilting lines are ¼″ apart. Five rows of parallel quilting lines, ¼″ apart, are also quilted on all sashing strips and white borders. Outline-quilt ¼″ inside seam lines of all white triangles of the sawtooth border.

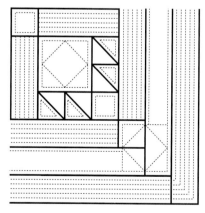

Quilting Diagram

Finished Edges
Bind quilt with blue print fabric.

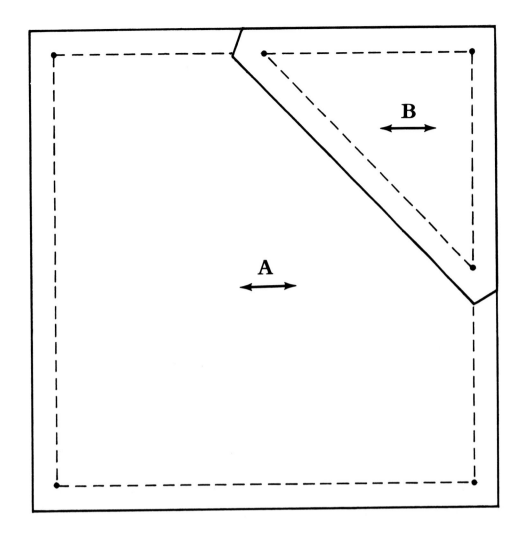

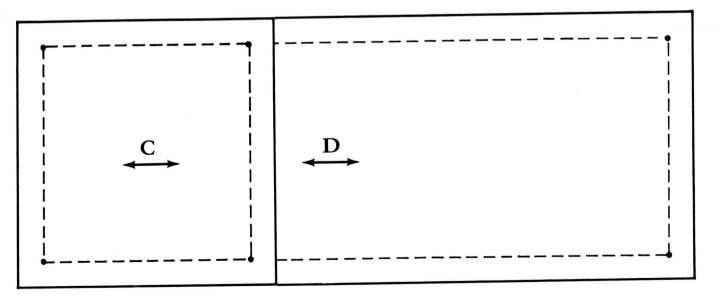

TRADITIONS
IN
QUILTING

Barbara Ellen Middy Russell (far left)
and Helen Louise Lindsey

Barbara Ellen Middy Russell & Helen Louise Lindsey

Urichsville and Piqua, Ohio

For many women who lived during the 19th century, sewing was an essential part of life. Barbara Ellen Middy Russell, who lived from 1835 to 1902, was recognized as an expert seamstress and quilter. Her first husband, George Francis Middy, fought in the Civil War and was the father of four of her five children. After his death she married a minister, John Russell. Barbara's dedication to fine hand sewing was a trait that was passed on to the generations of family members that followed.

Helen Louise Lindsey was Barbara's granddaughter and was born in her grandmother's home. She was educated at Miami University in Ohio and taught school for many years, primarily high school Latin. In the 1930s, she retired so that she could care for her mother, Louella.

Just as her mother had taught her, Louella Lindsey taught her daughter Helen to quilt as a young girl. It was during Helen's retirement years that she and her mother devoted many hours to fine hand sewing. They made a large number of quilts. Many were given as gifts, and others have remained in the family.

Several of these ladies' quilts were inherited by David Sanders, the great-great grandson of Barbara and the great-nephew of Helen. David is a banker who lives in Mobile, Alabama, in a restored 1859 Gulf Coast cottage. Much of the restoration of the cottage was done by David, with care not to damage the integrity of the original home and to preserve the original materials whenever possible. Barbara and Helen would be proud to know of his accomplishments and to know that their quilts have landed in the hands of a descendant who gives the quilts the same care and attention that the ladies themselves would have.

Whig Rose
1865

There must have been a celebration in 1865 when Barbara Middy's husband returned home from serving in the 51st Ohio Infantry during the Civil War. Long hours and days filled with wondering when and if loved ones would return home were now behind Barbara. Quilting had probably played an important role in passing the time and keeping her mind focused away from the war.

This quilt was made in 1865. Was it made in anticipation or in celebration of her husband's return? We can only speculate. Whichever was the case, there must have been gladness in her heart, and it shows in the bright and sunny colors that she chose. This quilt is special to family members and significant, too, because it is the only quilt made by Barbara that has survived through the years.

Whig Rose

Finished Quilt Size
77¼" x 77¼"

Number of Blocks and Finished Size
9 blocks—22" x 22"

Fabric Requirements

Green	— 3 yd.
Orange	— 2¼ yd.
Red print	— 2¼ yd.
Muslin	— 6¼ yd.★
Green for bias binding	— 1 yd.
Backing	— 4⅝ yd.

★If muslin is 45" wide or more, it is possible to cut two 22½" squares per row; in this case 4⅓ yd., instead of 6¼ yd., would be required. (See steps 1 and 7.)

Number to Cut★★

Template A	—9 red print
Template B	—36 green
Template C	—36 green
Template D	—144 green
Template E	—36 green
Template F	—36 green
Template G	—72 red print
Template H	—72 orange
Template I	—144 red print
Template J	—144 orange

★★See steps 4, 5, and 6 before cutting fabrics.

Quilt Top Assembly

1. Cut nine 22½" squares from muslin. Finger-crease each square on the diagonal; then finger-crease again on the opposite diagonal to find center and to form guidelines for appliqué. Layer appliqué squares with pieces A through I, as shown in Placement Diagrams.

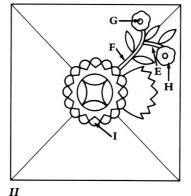

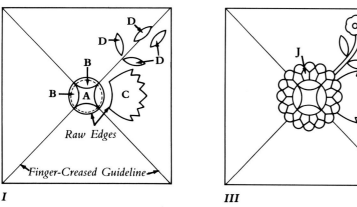

Placement Diagrams

2. Join 16 pieces (J) to form a circle. Appliqué circle to block, as shown.
3. Join 3 blocks at sides to form a row. Make 3 rows. Join rows.
4. Cut 4 border strips, 1⅜" wide, from green. Join to quilt and miter corners.
5. Cut 4 border strips, 1⅜" wide, from red print. Join to quilt and miter corners.
6. Cut 4 border strips, 1⅜" wide, from orange. Join to quilt and miter corners.
7. Cut 4 borders, 3½" wide, from muslin. Join to quilt and miter corners.

Quilting
Quilt across blocks with a 1" diagonal cross-hatching pattern. Border strips and borders are quilted in diagonal triads, ⅝" apart, containing quilting lines, ¼" apart.

Finished Edges
Bind with green fabric.

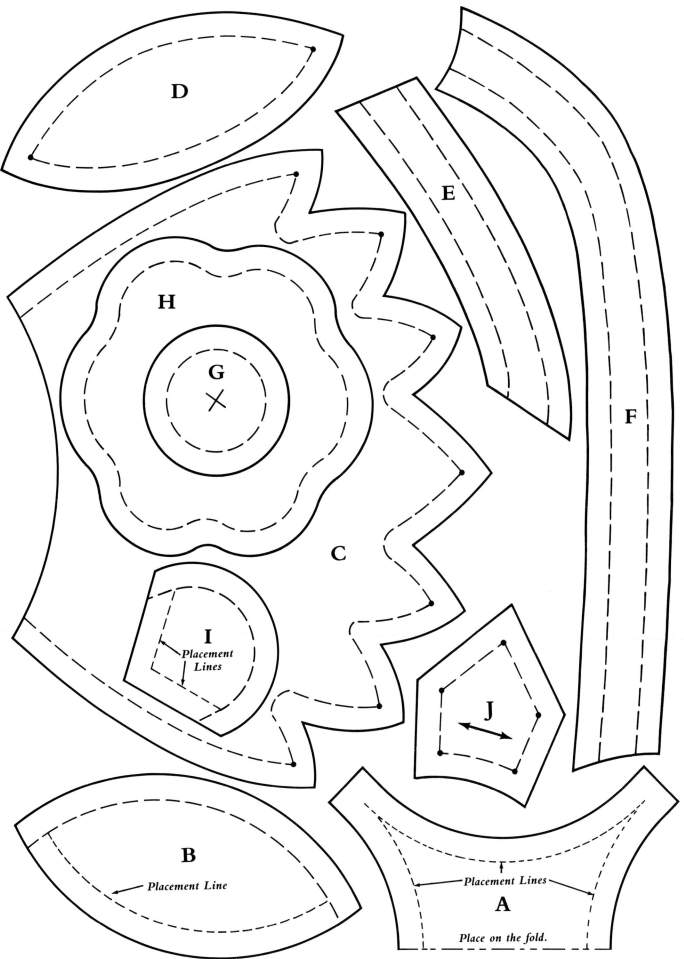

D

E

F

H

G

C

I

*Placement
Lines*

J

B

Placement Line

Placement Lines

A

Place on the fold.

111

Cherry
1935

Clusters of cherries, believed to be the symbols for sweet character and good works, were popular motifs among appliqué quilters throughout the United States, especially during the era of the Baltimore Album Quilts. Cherries embellished floral wreaths, cornucopias, baskets, and various other designs. Here clusters of them stand alone in a radiant splash of color and symmetry.

Helen Louise Lindsey's adeptness in fine needlework is represented in every cherry. Each is round, of equal size, and lies flat, and each cherry is evenly spaced in relation to the next one. It is believed that her mother, Louella, assisted her in some fashion with all of her quilts.

The rows and rows of cross-hatched quilting over this large quilt make it a noteworthy quilting feat. Oh, by the way, this is one of two identical quilts!

Cherry

Finished Quilt Size
96″ x 113″

Number of Blocks and Finished Size
20 blocks—17″ x 17″

Fabric Requirements
Red	—2 yd.
Green	—2½ yd.
Muslin	—9½ yd.
Muslin for bias binding	—1¼ yd.
Backing	—9¾ yd.

Number to Cut
Template A	—840 red
Template B	—240 green
Template B★	—240 green
Template C	—120 green

★Flip or turn over template if fabric is one-sided.

Quilt Top Assembly

1. Cut twenty 17½″ squares from muslin. Place cherries (A) and leaves (B) on squares, as shown in Placement Diagram and in detail photograph of quilt, and appliqué. Note that the cherry placement leaves a space of muslin, approximately 5″ square, in the center. Appliqué stems (C), as shown.

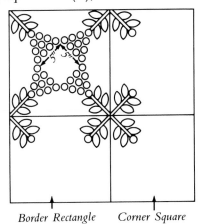

Border Rectangle   Corner Square

Placement Diagram

2. Join 4 blocks at sides to form a row. Make 5 rows. Join rows.
3. Cut 18 rectangles, 14½″ x 17½″, from muslin. Cut four 14½″ squares from muslin for corners.

Appliqué with cherries, leaves, and stems, as shown in Placement Diagram and in quilt photograph.
4. Join 5 appliquéd rectangles at sides to form a border. Make 2. Refer to quilt photograph for border placement and join to sides of quilt.
5. Join 4 appliquéd rectangles each, as before, to form borders for top and bottom of quilt. Join an appliquéd square to each end. Refer to

quilt photograph for border placement and join to top and bottom of quilt.

Quilting
The entire quilt is background-quilted with a 1″ diagonal cross-hatching pattern.

Finished Edges
Bind with muslin.

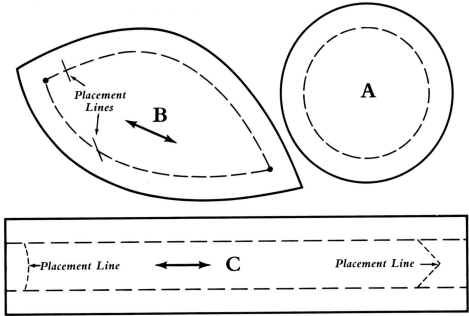

Elizabeth values her childhood days, growing up on a farm in western Kentucky. They were days filled with learning a mixed bag of skills in which she is still proficient today. Canning, sewing, crocheting, knitting, and quilting were just a few of the essentials that she was taught by her family. "I was an apprentice to them all as a child," says Elizabeth. Her mother quilted regularly, and with her guidance Elizabeth made her first quilt, a four-patch, when she was twelve. "I have a doll lunch cloth and napkins that I embroidered and hemmed when I was six years old," remembers Elizabeth. "And as a teenager, I completed a Dutch Doll quilt." Needlework, in periods of varying intensity, continued to be a part of Elizabeth's life. "Since retirement," says Elizabeth, "I have renewed my interest in quilts and am excited about the projects ahead."

Elizabeth R. Lawrence
Athens, Georgia

Cathedral Window
1986
Quilters should pause to bask in the magnificent feat of hand needlework executed by the maker of a Cathedral Window coverlet. Elizabeth's *Cathedral Window* embodies two years of meticulous hand stitches. Her attention to detail yielded the smooth, pristine curves of every window that make her *Cathedral Window* exceptional.

Technically, the Cathedral Window design does not fit the definition of a quilt since it does not have any padding or backing, but quilters have readily adopted it into their family of favorite designs. Our instructions are written for hand piecing, though a Cathedral Window may also be machine-pieced.

Cathedral Window

Finished Quilt Size
81" x 99"

Number of Blocks and Finished Size
99 blocks—9" x 9"

Fabric Requirements
Unbleached muslin — 29¼ yd.
Blue/gray print   — 4¾ yd.

Quilt Top Assembly
1. Cut 891 seven-inch squares from muslin. Make a 6"-square template. Lay template on muslin square, turn ½" seam allowance over edges of template, and press.
2. Fold square in half, right sides together, with seam allowance folded down as pressed. With close overcast stitches, sew edges together at sides from *open* edge down 1½" or halfway down, as shown in Diagram I. (Lower portion of the sides will be left open.)

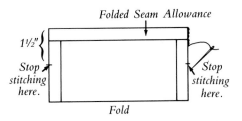

Folded Seam Allowance

1½"

Stop stitching here.

Stop stitching here.

Fold

Diagram I

3. Turn piece right side out and match seam lines, as shown in Diagram II. Fold back along open edge. Using a slipstitch, sew edges together, beginning at center seam and stitching 1½" on either side. Or begin 1½" from end, as shown. (Slipstitching is a total of 3".) Flatten into a 4½" square.

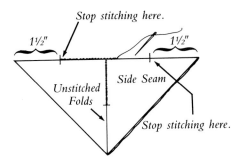

Stop stitching here.

1½"

1½"

Unstitched Folds

Side Seam

Stop stitching here.

Diagram II

4. Turn square over so that unsewn side is on top. Bring two opposite corners together and tack, as shown in Diagram III. Bring the remaining two corners together and tack. Then tack at center through *all* thicknesses. Square should equal 3".

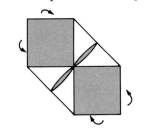

Diagram III

5. With needle and unknotted thread, make a double stitch at each corner, catching unstitched fold on each side. Leave a 1" tail of thread on both ends. This ensures sharp corners and makes assembling the squares much easier. This thread can be removed once the squares are joined.

6. Arrange squares in 3 rows of 3 squares each. Join squares at sides to form a row and join rows to complete a 9-square block. Make 99 blocks.
7. Cut 1,722 two-inch squares from blue/gray print for windows. Pin window square over the diamond shape formed by the unstitched edges of two adjoining squares, as shown in Diagram IV. Fold muslin edge over the window square. Slip-stitch in place, leaving ¼" un-stitched on each end of seam. Bar-tack each corner for reinforcement. Continue in this manner for all blocks. Elizabeth recommends inserting the window squares before the blocks are joined into rows to avoid having to handle the whole quilt.
8. Arrange blocks in 9 rows of 11 blocks each. Join blocks at sides to form a row. As blocks are joined, insert window squares in the diamonds that are formed. Join rows and insert remaining window squares as before.

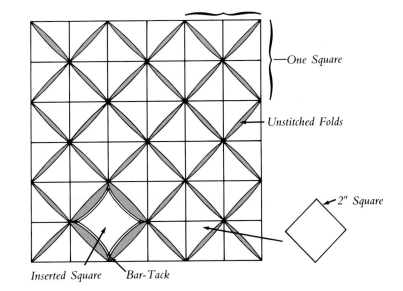

—One Square

—Unstitched Folds

2" Square

Inserted Square   *Bar-Tack*

Diagram IV

Angeline Lewis Pond and
Hattie Pond Fleming (above right)

Angeline Lewis Pond & Hattie Pond Fleming

Wells Bridge, New York

They came from a generation of utility quilters. A generation that required quick bedcovers for cold snowy nights, like those in up-state New York. Angeline Pond and her daughter Hattie had many parallels in their lives. Both were handy with the needle and excellent quilters, both married dairy farmers, and both of their husbands died in the same year, 1895, only a few months apart.

Barbara and Frank Harwood
Red Bank, New Jersey

After losing their husbands, the mother and daughter were once again living under the same roof. It is highly probable that, during the winter, Angeline and Hattie worked on many quilts together, and sometimes with Hattie's three daughters. Several of the quilts made by Angeline and Hattie were left to Frank and Barbara Harwood by his mother, Blanche, who was Hattie's daughter.

Barbara Harwood, an accomplished quilter and quilt teacher herself, cherishes one particular afternoon that she spent with Blanche. Rummaging through a family trunk, Blanche pulled out a few of the quilts that Angeline and Hattie had made. "I was thrilled," says Barbara. Among them were *Prairie Star* and *Rail Fence II* (see below). "They are such a treasure to us," says Barbara. "May they be enjoyed and appreciated by everyone for many generations to come."

Prairie Star

1880-1890s

Howdy, partner! Got your sewing guns loaded and ready? Let's head for the prairie and shoot a star, a *Prairie Star*.

Hattie's daughter Blanche remembers her Grandmother Pond working on this quilt. *Prairie Star* contains numerous pieces, set-in piecing, and heaps of quilting. These are pattern and quilting distinctions that are most often attributed to quilts made by experienced quilters. And at the time Angeline Pond made this quilt, she would certainly have been considered an experienced quilter.

The bar construction, seen so often in star quilts of this period, requires accurate set-in piecing. The angular double sawtooth borders complement the porcupine-like circles created by the color placement within the star pattern.

Prairie Star

Finished Quilt Size
73½" x 82"

Fabric Requirements
Red — 2½ yd.
White — 4¾ yd.
Red for bias
  binding — 1 yd.
Backing — 4¾ yd.

Number to Cut
Template A   — 480 red
                    384 white
Template B★   — 164 red
                    164 white
Template C   — 19 white
Template D   — 14 white
12½" square   — 6 white
12½" x 6½"
  rectangle   — 10 white
★Some quilters may prefer the
quick machine-piecing method for
pieced squares. See step 4 before
cutting fabric.

Quilt Top Assembly
1. Alternate colors and join diamonds (A) at sides in sets of three,
as shown in Star Piecing Diagram.
Join sets to form 8 large diamonds.
Join large diamonds to form a star.
Make 12 stars.

Star Piecing Diagram

2. Arrange triangles (D) and squares
(C) between stars, as shown in
Row Assembly Diagram. Join to
form a row. Make 4 rows.

Row Assembly Diagram

To sew these triangles and
squares between the star points,
begin stitching from seam line of
outside edge to seam line of inside
edge. Stop and backstitch 1 or 2
stitches. Remove fabric from machine. Align the remaining sides
and stitch from the center to the
seam line of outside edge, back-
stitching 1 or 2 stitches at the start.
3. Join rows by setting in 6½" x
12½" rectangles and 12½" squares,
as shown in Setting Diagram I. Set
in corner squares (C), triangles (D),

and rectangles, as shown, to complete top and bottom edges.
4. Join all white triangles (B) to all
red triangles (B) to form pieced
squares.

Or, for the quick machine-piecing
method for pieced squares, lay two
fabric rectangles (one white and one
red) of equal size, with right sides
together, and red on the bottom.
Mark a grid of 2⅞" squares on the
top fabric. Draw a diagonal line
through each square. Machine-stitch
¼" on either side of diagonal lines.

Setting Diagram I

Setting Diagram II

(See Pieced Squares Diagram.) Cut along marked lines.

Join 41 squares at sides 4 times to form 4 rows.

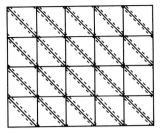

Pieced Squares Diagram

5. Cut 2 strips, 2½″ wide, from white. Join a row of triangles to each side of strip, as shown in Setting Diagram II, twice. Join to sides of quilt.

Quilting
Angeline Pond outline-quilted ¼″ inside seam lines of star pieces, squares, rectangles, and triangles. Outline-quilting from star points extends horizontally across connecting squares to meet the outline-quilting of the next star. The same is done across the 12″ connecting squares and rectangles from all star points. (See quilt photograph.) A zigzag pattern is quilted on the 2″ white border strip.

Finished Edges
Bind with red fabric.

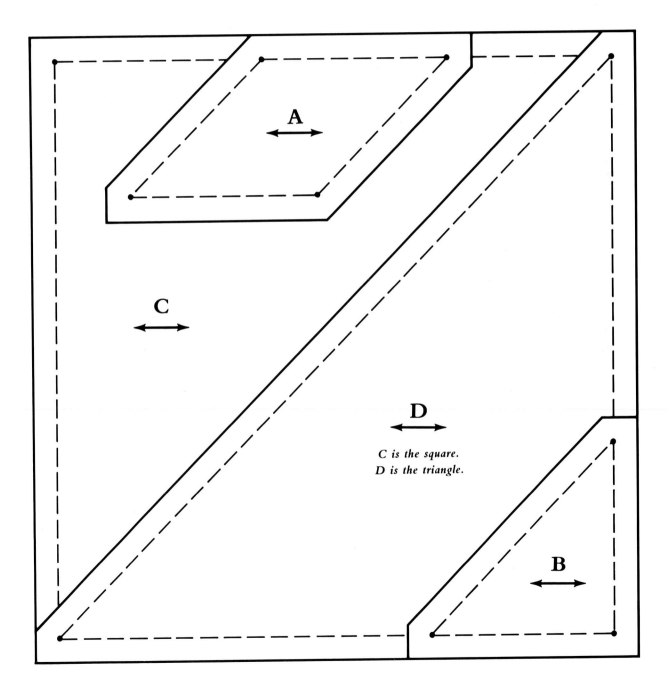

C is the square.
D is the triangle.

Rail Fence II
1880–1890s

Rail Fence II fits all the criteria of a utility quilt. It has essentially one pattern piece, it's easy to piece, it's very likely that it was made from fabric on hand, and it's tied and tufted for expediency.

It is not certain who made the quilt, Angeline or Hattie or both, but it is certain that the maker knew how to tie a quilt. The knots and the tufting are still intact and in remarkably good condition.

120

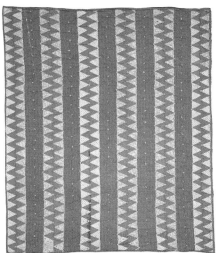

Rail Fence II

Finished Quilt Size
71½″ x 81″

Fabric Requirements
Pink   —6 yd.
White   —3⅝ yd.
Pink for bias
  binding   —1 yd.
Backing   —4¾ yd.

Other Materials
Thread, high-twist, sturdy, white
Yarn, high-loft, 4-ply, man-made
  fiber, white
Needle, darning size 15

Number to Cut
Template A —318 pink
               318 white
Template B —12 pink
               12 white

Quilt Top Assembly
1. Alternate pink triangles (A and B) with white triangles (A and B) and join at sides, as shown in Rail Piecing Diagram. Make 6 Rail As and 6 Rail Bs.

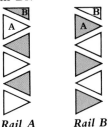

Rail A   *Rail B*
Rail Piecing Diagram

2. Join Rail As to Rail Bs, as shown in Setting Diagram I.
3. Cut 5 panels, 7″ wide, from pink. Alternate rails with panels, as shown in Setting Diagram II, and join.

Rail A
← Rail B

Setting Diagram I   *Setting Diagram II*

Tufting
Refer to Tuft Placement Diagram and pin-baste quilt layers at each spot that will be tied. Thread needle with approximately 10″ of sturdy thread and leave unknotted. Insert needle through all layers at the spot that will be tied and make a backstitch over pin. Leave a 3″ tail. Backstitch over same place one more time. Clip thread, leaving a 3″ tail. Tie tails into a square knot, as shown in Diagram I.

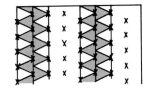

Tuft Placement Diagram

Diagram I

For tufts, cut three 2″ strands of yarn. Center over square knot and anchor strands with another square knot, as shown in Diagram II.

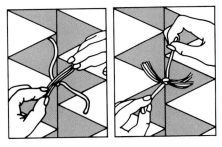

Diagram II

Finished Edges
Bind with pink fabric.

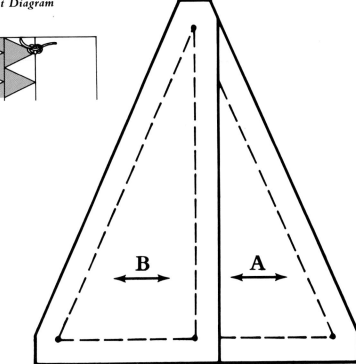

B ←→   A ←→

BEE
QUILTERS

Working on another fabulous fund-raising quilt are (seated, left to right)—*Jenny Perry, Sherrie Allen, Mary Zimmerman, Alice Heath, Eunice Harper, Ruby Mauk, Su Bachert, and* (standing, left to right)—*Starr Kaiser and Marie Salazar.*

Kentucky Heritage Quilt Society

Lexington, Kentucky

In less than a decade, the Kentucky Heritage Quilt Society has grown to more than 300 members, some from nearly every county in the state. It is the first statewide organization in the Commonwealth of Kentucky to be concerned with all aspects of quilting.

The society conducts regular quilt contests, shows, and workshops throughout the state. It takes pride in its Kentucky Documentation Program and Quilters on File, an archive of interviews with Kentucky's quiltmakers. General meetings are held two or three times a year, and they feature a program with quilt-related activities, such as workshops, lectures, or demonstrations.

Ryder's Star
1986

Usually the quilters go to the quilt, but in Kentucky the quilt goes to the quilters. It could be said that *Ryder's Star* probably has more mileage on it than a teenager's first car.

The reason, though, is justifiable and certainly honorable. So that every member throughout the state of Kentucky can participate in the society's annual fund-raising quilt project, a request for volunteer piecers is made via the society's newsletter. "The response to piece for *Ryder's Star* was so overwhelming," remembers the quilt's designer Nancy Ryder, "that I had more requests than I had blocks or border units!" For this quilt, block packets with directions were compiled and mailed by Nancy, and all completed blocks were returned to her within a few months. Once the top was pieced and basted, the quilt traveled around the state to be quilted by various guilds and bees.

Society members who worked on *Ryder's Star* are Sherrie Allen, Winona Asher, Su Bachert, Verna Broaddus, Ann Brotzke, Jane Brown, Mary Pat Carroll, Nellie Charlton, Edith Chumley, Lorraine Dickhaus, Sarah Frye, Lois Gardner, Elsie Harmon, Eunice Harper, Alice Heath, Pauline Hurst, Mary Jewett, Starr Kaiser, Mary Lucas, Ruby Mauk, Alida McLain, Betty Jo Meador, Lillian Molen, Priscilla Munson, Mary Neusel, Jenny Perry, Barbara Quinn, Kathleen Ramsey, Marjorie Rose, Nancy Ryder, Kate Rye, Kathleen Rye, Marie Salazar, Judy Scott, Twyla Sheffield, Helen Thompson, Frances Williams, Eva Wilson, and Mary Zimmerman.

The following quilters are members of affiliated guilds who worked on the quilt when it was in their area of the state. They are Ethel Boggs, Ruth Boggs, Janet Cloud, Bernice Henderson, Nancy Justice, Lucy Sperry, Marilla Stringer, and Carrie Vanbibber.

Ryder's Star

Finished Quilt Size
85″ x 85″

Number of Blocks and Finished Size
13 Block 1—15″ x 15″
12 Block 2—15″ x 15″

Fabric Requirements
Med. blue with
  white dots (MB) — 1¾ yd.
Blue/rose floral
  print (BRF) — 1⅛ yd.
Navy print — 2¼ yd.
Lt. blue print
  on white (LBP) — 1¼ yd.
Navy floral
  stripe (NFS) — 1⅞ yd.
Maroon print — 1¾ yd.
Wine print
  on white (WP) — ¾ yd.
Muslin — 1⅝ yd.
Navy print for bias
  binding — 1¼ yd.
Backing — 5 yd.

Number to Cut
Template A — 13 MB
Template B — 72 MB
            72 NFS
Template C — 52 BRF
            112 navy print
            60 LBP
            48 NFS
            136 maroon print
            48 WP
            60 muslin
Template D — 52 MB
Template E — 48 BRF
            104 LBP
Template F — 48 muslin
Template G — 20 navy print

Quilt Top Assembly
1. Referring to Piecing Diagram for Block 1 and colored block drawing, join LBP triangles (E) to sides of

square (D). Join MB triangle (B) to form a pieced square, as shown. Make 4 pieced squares.

Join 4 triangles (C) to form a pieced square, as shown. Make 4. Arrange pieced squares and square (A) into sections, as shown, and join sections. Make 13 of Block 1.

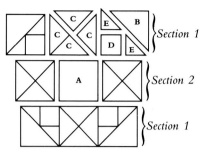

Piecing Diagram for Block 1

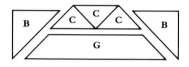

2. Referring to Piecing Diagram for Block 2 and colored block drawing, join pieces E, F, and B to form a

Piecing Diagram for Block 2

pieced square. Make 4.

Join 4 triangles (C), noting fabric arrangement, to form a pieced square. Make 5. Arrange pieced squares into sections, as shown, and join sections. Make 12 of Block 2.

3. Alternate 3 Block 1s with 2 Block 2s to form a row. (See quilt photograph.) Join blocks at sides and make 3 rows.

Alternate 3 Block 2s with 2 Block 1s to form a row. Join blocks at sides and make 2 rows.

Alternate rows and join. (See quilt photograph.)

4. Referring to Border Piecing Diagram and colored drawings, join triangles (B and C) and piece (G) to form border unit. Make 8 units with MB triangles (B) and one muslin triangle (C) in center, as shown. Make 12 units with NFS triangles (B) and one LBP triangle (C) in the center. (See quilt photograph.)

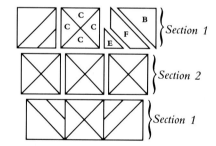

Border Piecing Diagram

Alternate 3 units with NFS triangles with 2 units with MB triangles. Join at sides to form border. Make 4 borders. Join 2 borders to sides of quilt with piece (G) on outside edge.

Join 2 navy print triangles (C), as shown in Corner Square Piecing Diagram. Join to MB triangle (B) to form corner square. Make 4 squares. Join a square to each end of remaining borders. (See quilt photograph for proper position of square.) Join borders to quilt.

Corner Square Piecing Diagram

Quilting

Outline-quilt ¼″ inside seam line of all block pieces. The Kentucky Heritage quilters quilted along the pattern of the print of the navy floral stripe and repeated that design on the MB triangles and squares. Outline-quilt ¼″ inside seam line of the base of all triangles and piece G in the borders. Quilt a line 1″ from that line and parallel to it.

Finished Edges

Bind with navy print fabric.

Quilt Documentation

Quilt name, guild name, date, quilt designer, and owner were typed on a piece of muslin and stitched to the back of *Ryder's Star*. (See photograph of quilt documentation.)

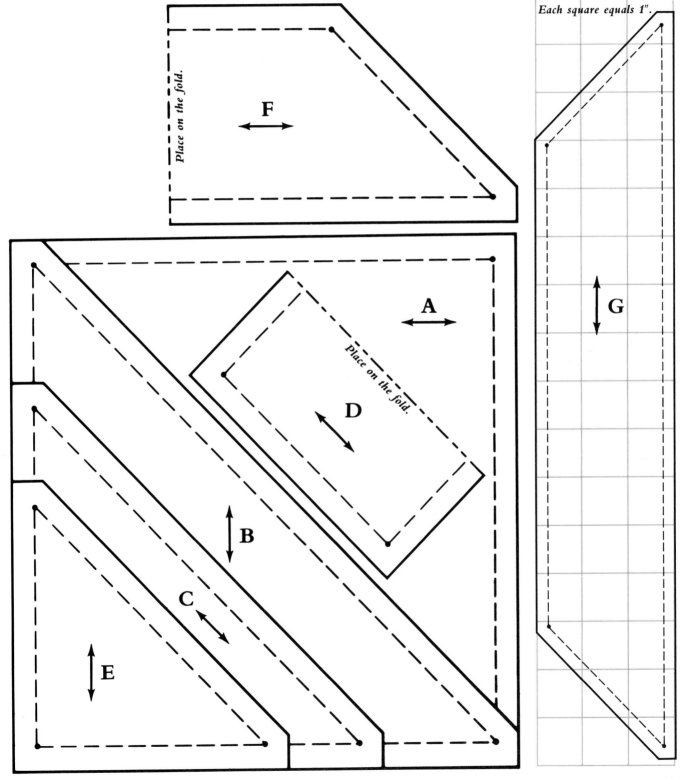

127

Jean Roberts (right), founder of the Midland Quilters Guild, prepares to do some quilting, as Pat Brooks (left) looks on.

Midland Quilters Guild

Midland, Texas

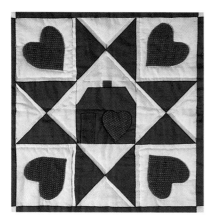

Ohio Star with Houses
1988

Symbolic of the love that permeates the walls of the Ronald McDonald House in Odessa, Texas, are the twenty-five hearts that enliven this Ohio Star pattern. Midland Quilters Guild member Pat Brown designed this modification of the Ohio Star block for the quilt block contest.

Pat Brooks was the originator of the wonderful paper doll boys-and-girls-with-hearts quilting pattern. Assisting the two Pats with hand-piecing, hand-appliquéing, and quilting was Jean Roberts.

One thing is almost certain if you are a member of the Midland Quilters Guild—you will find it hard to excuse yourself from attending its meetings. To accommodate the various schedules of its members, the guild is divided into four chapters and two quilting bees. Chapters meet once a month on Monday evenings, Tuesday mornings, Tuesday evenings, and Wednesday afternoons.

The membership of more than 100 sponsors a quilt show every other year. They also participate in quilting demonstrations and programs for the public and interested community groups, and donate books on quilt-related topics to the public library.

The quilt featured here was made from blocks that the members of the Midland Guild had entered in a quilt block contest sponsored by a fellow guild in Odessa, Texas. (Odessa is some 20 miles from Midland.) The purpose of the contest was to design a block that would be used to make a quilt for the new Ronald McDonald House in Odessa. Contest rules stipulated that the red pindot fabric furnished by the Odessa guild must be used and that a heart pattern must appear somewhere in the design.

A member of the Midland Quilters Guild won first prize: 21 of the blocks that had been entered in the contest. With the thought of returning these blocks to the sick children, guild members were asked to piece the blocks into small quilts. By the fall of 1988, 35 items, including lap quilts, crib quilts, wall hangings, and pillows, were presented to the house.

Ohio Star with Houses

Finished Quilt Size
47¾" x 47¾"

Number of Blocks and Finished Size
5 blocks—12¾" x 12¾"

Fabric Requirements
Blue	—2 yd.
Red with white pindots*	—1½ yd.**
Solid red	—¼ yd.
White	—1 yd.
Backing	—3 yd.

*Throughout the directions,

red with white pindots will be designated as red.
**Includes yardage for binding.

Other Materials
Freezer paper
Fabric-compatible glue stick

Number to Cut
Template A	—40 white
	40 blue
Template B	—20 white
Template C	—5 blue
Template D	—5 white
Template E	—5 blue
Template F	—5 solid red
Template G	—5 solid red

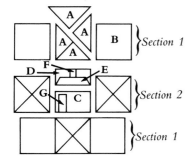

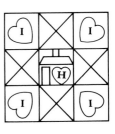

Block Appliqué Diagram

3. Cut four 13¼″ squares from blue. Alternate 2 pieced blocks with 1 blue square to form a row. Make 2 rows. Alternate 2 blue squares with 1 pieced block to form a row. Refer to quilt photograph and join rows.

4. Cut 2 border strips, 1½″ wide, from red. Join to top and bottom of quilt. Cut 2 border strips, 1½″ wide, from red. Join to sides of quilt.

5. Cut 2 borders, 4¼″ wide, from blue. Join to top and bottom of quilt. Cut 2 borders, 4¼″ wide, from blue. Join to sides of quilt.

Quilting

Outline-quilt ¼″ inside seam line of all white triangles and squares, as shown in Quilting Diagram. Outline-quilt around each heart. Quilt the paper doll boys-and-girls-with-hearts pattern in each blue block, using white quilting thread. Quilt a heart in the center of each. Outline-quilt ¼″ inside seam lines of red border. Alternate positions of hearts and quilt on blue border. (See quilt photograph.)

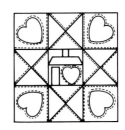

Quilting Diagram

Finished Edges

Cut 4 binding strips, 2¼″ wide, from red. Fold and press binding strips in half lengthwise. Match raw edges and stitch to front of quilt, including both raw edges of binding in seam. Turn binding to back of quilt, mitering corners, and blindstitch in place along folded edge.

Quilt Top Assembly

1. Join blue triangles (A) to white triangles (A) to form a pieced square, as shown in Block Piecing Diagram. Make 4. Join squares (B) to opposite sides of 2 pieced squares to form section 1s, as shown.

Block Piecing Diagram

Using placement lines, appliqué chimney (F) and roof (E) to rectangle (D), as shown in Block Piecing Diagram. Appliqué door (G) to rectangle (C). Join rectangles (C, D) to form center square, as shown. Join pieced squares to opposite sides to form section 2. Join sections. Make 5 blocks.

2. Appliqué hearts (H, I) to blocks, as shown in Block Appliqué Diagram. Trace heart onto dull side of freezer paper. Cut on traced line. Iron shiny side to red fabric, lining up with fabric grain lines as appropriate for design. Cut fabric, leaving at least a ¼″ seam allowance. Turn seam allowance to back side of paper and stick down with fabric glue. Clip inside corners and curves as necessary. The point of a pin or toothpick may be helpful to adjust gathers on back of outside curves so that the edge will be smooth. Place heart in position. Use masking tape to anchor piece in place and appliqué.

Repeat procedure for all hearts and position them, as shown in Block Appliqué Diagram. Cut fabric from behind each heart. Soak piece in warm water to soften glue, if necessary, and ease out freezer paper. Dry flat and press.

129

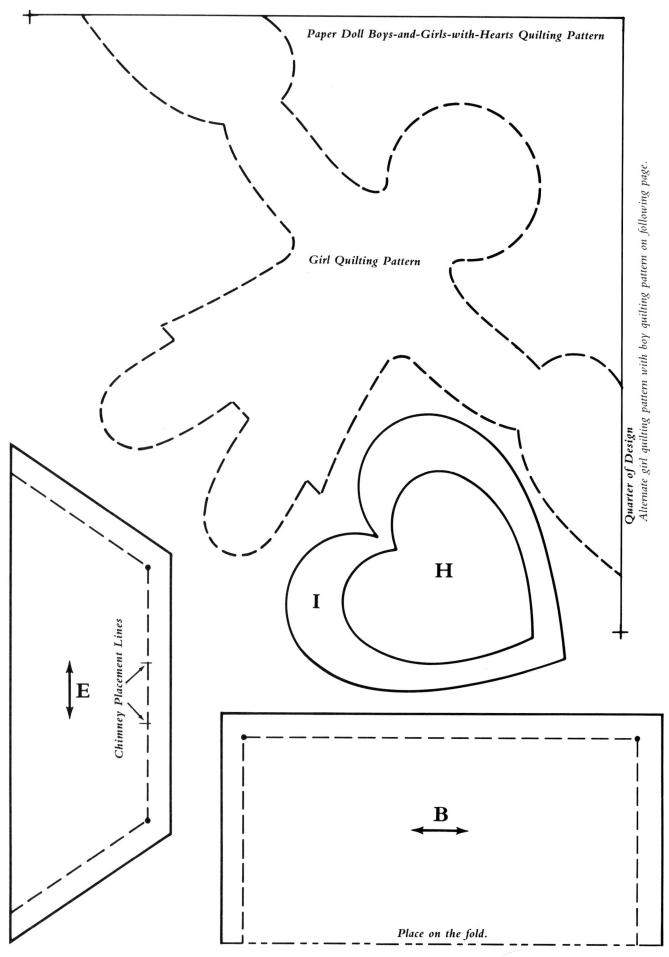

Paper Doll Boys-and-Girls-with-Hearts Quilting Pattern

Girl Quilting Pattern

Quarter of Design
Alternate girl quilting pattern with boy quilting pattern on following page.

H

I

Chimney Placement Lines

E

B

Place on the fold.

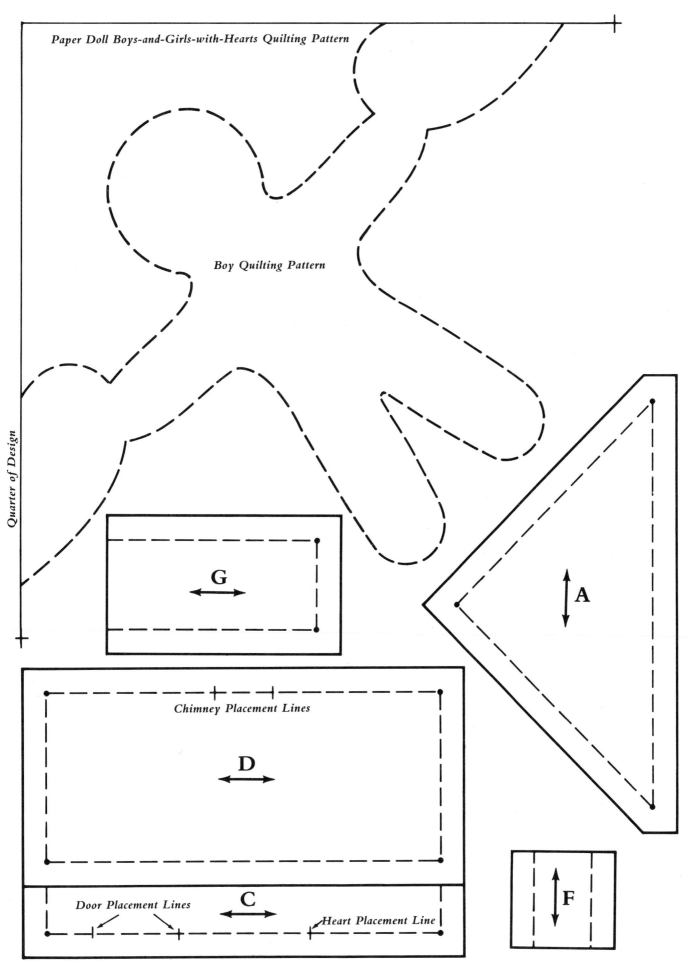

Paper Doll Boys-and-Girls-with-Hearts Quilting Pattern

Boy Quilting Pattern

Quarter of Design

G

A

Chimney Placement Lines

D

C

F

Door Placement Lines

Heart Placement Line

Posing in front of 1,001 Nights are some of its makers (seated, left to right)—Edith Zimmer, Irene Terhaar, and (standing, left to right)—Margie Potter, Patti Garretson, Lynn Johnson, Pat Faddis, Donna Rasmussen, and Arlene Stamper.

Quilt San Diego

San Diego, California

Every person who belongs to a guild in San Diego also belongs to Quilt San Diego. Quilt San Diego is a nonprofit organization dedicated to the education of quiltmakers and the appreciation of quiltmaking as an art form. It also provides a source of challenge and inspiration to quiltmakers through the promotion of juried shows. Quilt San Diego has no membership dues or monthly newsletters. An 11-member board meets regularly to plan exhibitions and to develop other ideas for promoting quiltmaking.

In all, Quilt San Diego encompasses 11 guilds. Once a year there is a multiguild meeting that features a national speaker, financed by voluntary contributions of one dollar from each guild member. Arlene Stamper, president of Quilt San Diego, tells us that the cooperation and camaraderie among the groups have been extremely beneficial to the advancement of quiltmaking in the San Diego area. Their first juried show in 1987 was a complete success, and plans for their second juried show, to be held in 1990, Visions—A New Decade, began shortly after their first show ended.

1,001 Nights
1988

Perhaps if Scheherezade of the *Arabian Nights* stories had had this beautiful quilt, her husband, Schariar, would never have thought of killing her.

Edith Zimmer, the stimulus behind *1,001 Nights*, was asked by Quilt San Diego board members to design a quilt as a fund-raiser for their second juried show. She was inspired by a quilt she saw in Georgia Bonesteel's book, *New Ideas for Lap Quilting*, which combined the blocks Fifty-four Forty or Fight and a variation of Star Daze. (See "Resources.") Quilters will find Edith's method for curved-border piecing, as seen here, quite easy.

Members from various guilds in San Diego assisted Edith with the piecing and quilting. They were Sharyn Craig, Pat Faddis, Patti Garretson, Lynn Johnson, Carol O'Brien, Margie Potter, Donna Rasmussen, Arlene Stamper, Irene Terhaar, and Rose Turner.

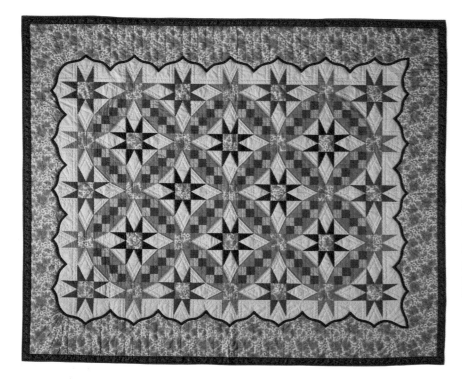

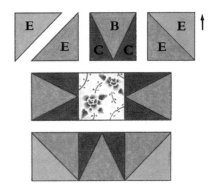

Block Piecing Diagram II
Block 2—Make 8.

3. Referring to Block Piecing Diagrams and colored block drawings, make the number indicated of blocks 3, 4, and 5, as shown.

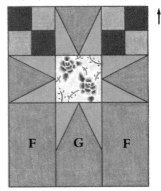

Block 3—Make 10.

1,001 Nights

Finished Quilt Size
84″ x 108″

Fabric Requirements
Gray — 4⅝ yd.
Blue — 2 yd.
Purple — 2½ yd.★
Cranberry — 1⅝ yd.
Lavender — ¾ yd.
Blue print — 4⅞ yd.
Paisley stripe — 3⅓ yd.★★
Cranberry for
  binding — 1¼ yd.
Backing — 9¼ yd.
★Includes yardage for bias strip.
★★More yardage will be needed if a multistripe fabric cannot be found.

Other Materials
Fabric-compatible glue stick
Celtic metal strips, ½″ wide

Number to Cut
Template A — 35 blue print★★★
Template B — 116 gray
Template C — 32 purple‡
  40 cranberry
  68 blue
Template C§ — 32 purple‡
  40 cranberry
  68 blue
Template D — 96 cranberry
  96 lavender
Template E — 48 gray
  48 blue
Template F — 40 gray

Template G — 24 gray
Template H — 4 gray
★★★Cut borders first. See step 5.
‡Cut pieces after making bias strip for border. See step 8.
§Flip or turn over template if fabric is one-sided.

Quilt Top Assembly
1. Join squares (A, D) and triangles (B, C), as shown in Block Piecing Diagram I. The diagram shows the colors for Block 1. Make 7.

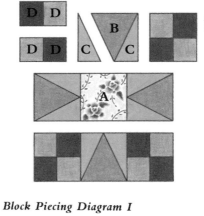

Block Piecing Diagram I
Block 1—Make 7.

■ *cranberry* ■ *gray* ■ *lavender*
▨ *blue print* ■ *purple* ▫ *blue*

2. Join square (A) and triangles (B, C, E), as shown in Block Piecing Diagram II. The diagram shows the colors for Block 2. Make 8.

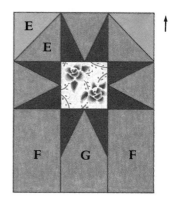

Block 4—Make 6.

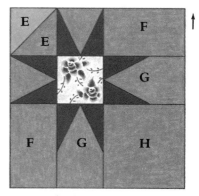

Block 5—Make 4.

4. Arrange blocks, as shown in Setting Diagram and quilt photograph. (Arrows indicate the top of each block.) Join blocks at sides to form rows and join rows.

5. Cut 4 borders for sides, 12" x 82½", from blue print. You will notice from the quilt photograph that the top border is narrower than the bottom border. That is because Edith was short of fabric when she made the quilt and had to make this adjustment. Therefore, her top corners are different from her bottom ones. (See quilt photograph.) *However, all borders are the same width for these instructions; therefore, all four corners of your quilt will be identical.*

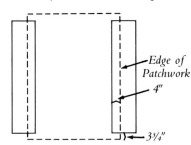

Setting Diagram

With right sides facing up, lay side borders on quilt so that they overlap 4" onto quilt patchwork, as shown in Border Assembly Diagram I. Center borders on sides of quilt, measuring carefully at intervals to assure that you have a 4" overlap. (There should be 3¾" of exposed patchwork on each end of the border.) Pin borders to quilt.

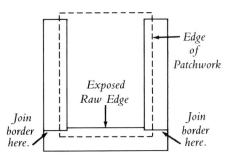

Border Assembly Diagram I

Place border guide ½" from inside border edge at center, as shown in Border Assembly Diagram II. Trace six on each side border. (There will be border fabric left unmarked on each end.)

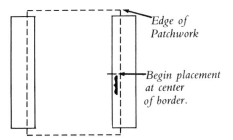

Border Assembly Diagram II

Pin generously along both sides of traced line. Topstitch directly on this line with a small-gauged stitch.
6. With *right sides together*, join top and bottom borders to side borders, as shown in Border Assembly Diagram III. Press seam allowances toward side borders. Raw edge of border in center will be exposed. Pin to patchwork.

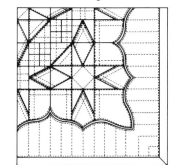

Border Assembly Diagram III

Place border guide ½" from inside border edge at center and trace four on each top and bottom border, as before. (See quilt photograph.) There will be border fabric left unmarked on each end.

Place border guide for corners and mark remaining border edges for corner treatment. (See quilt photograph.)

Pin and machine-stitch borders, as before.
7. Trim excess border fabric ⅛" from topstitching *on the patchwork side* (inside edge). Turn quilt over and trim excess patchwork ⅛" from the topstitching.
8. Make 1⅜"-wide bias strip from purple. With *wrong* sides together, fold strip lengthwise and stitch together with a ⅛" seam allowance. Using celtic metal strips, press with seam allowance down the center of the strip.
9. Using glue stick, tack bias strip along traced border design, centering it over topstitching, as shown in photograph of bias strip application. Miter at all points.

When strips are ready to be joined, cut the strip that is being glued at the end of a point in the border design. Fold the next strip under and over the first strip at a 90° angle and glue in place. (See photograph.)

Hand-appliqué both sides of bias strip to quilt.

10. Cut 4 border strips, 2¼" wide, from paisley stripe. Join to quilt and miter corners.

Quilting

Outline-quilt ¼" outside seam line of pieces, as shown in Quilting Diagram. Parallel lines of quilting on borders are 2" apart.

Quilting Diagram

Finished Edges

Bind with cranberry fabric.

Quilt Documentation

A piece of muslin with hand-printed paragraphs and frayed edging contains the documentation for *1,001 Nights*. (See photograph.) The paragraphs tell about the quilt's makers, designer, and owner. A small paragraph also gives suggestions for the care of the quilt.

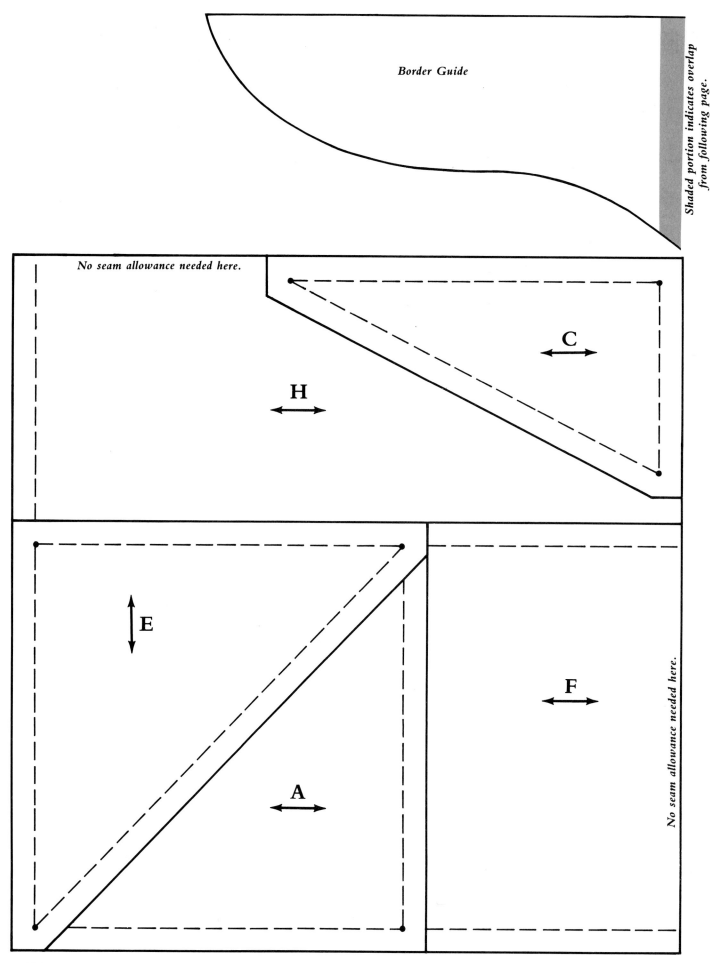

Border Guide

Shaded portion indicates overlap from following page.

No seam allowance needed here.

H

C

E

A

F

No seam allowance needed here.

136

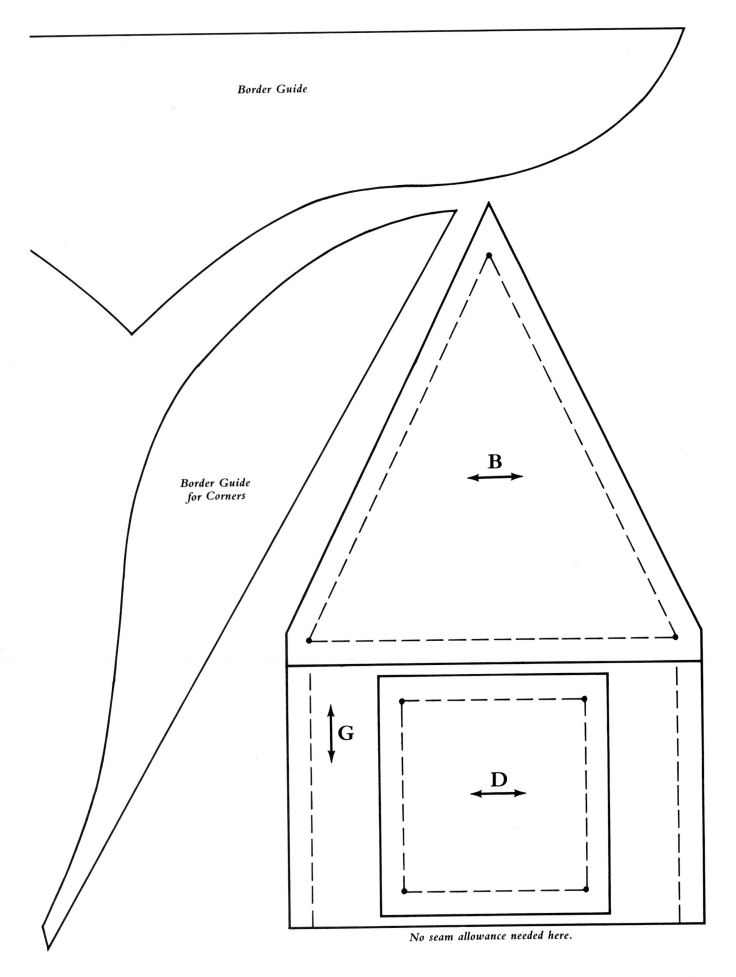

Border Guide

Border Guide for Corners

B

G

D

No seam allowance needed here.

137

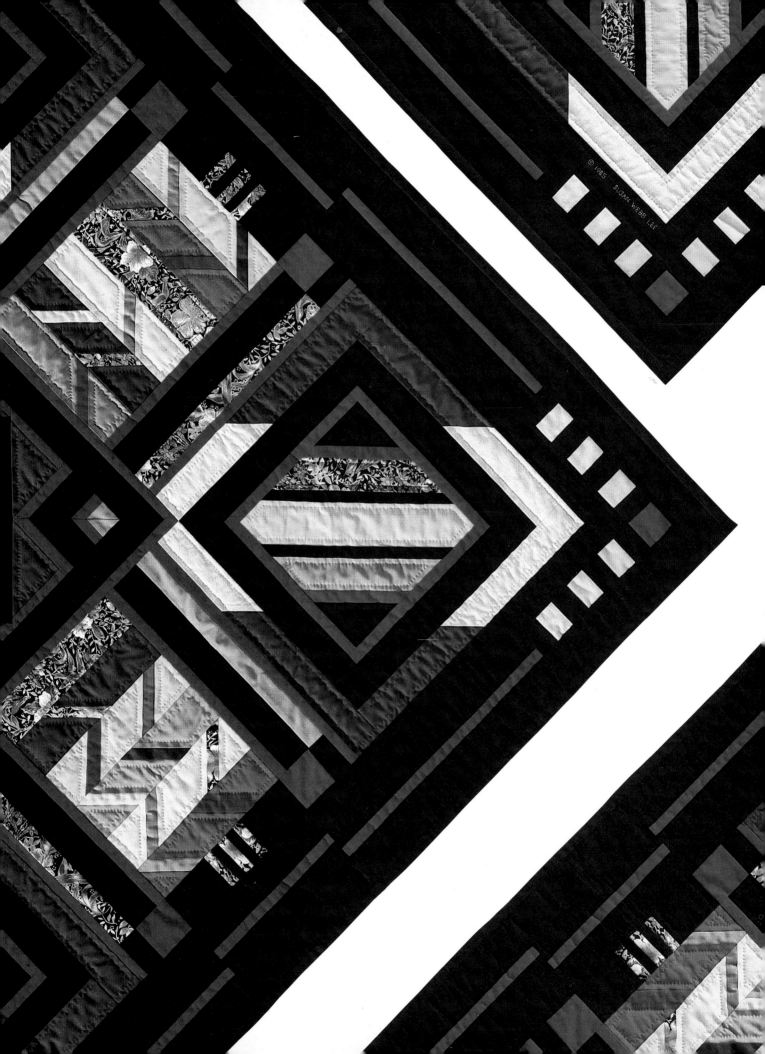
© 1985 SUSAN WEBB LEE

DESIGNER GALLERY

"I make quilts in every conceivable way!" says Dixie. A quilter for over 20 years, she finds that all phases of quiltmaking afford an unending challenge and excitement. Quilting per se is especially appealing to her because of its meditative quality.

Dixie remains active in her local guild, the Pensacola Quilters Guild, as well as in fulfilling the demands of teaching all over the country. Her quilts are generally original designs, such as seen below and in her quilt *Hoshi Sensu* in our "Starmakers" chapter.

Dixie Haywood
Pensacola, Florida

Fruit of the Bloom
1984

Full of personal symbolism, *Fruit of the Bloom* is a cherished possession of Dixie and her husband, Bob. Before Dixie made the quilt, Bob had suffered a heart attack and was in need of a little encouragement. Recognizing the importance of laughter in the healing process, Dixie conceived the idea of making a quilt dedicated to Bob's addiction to watermelons. "I realized," says she, "that over the years I had permanently lost a shelf in my refrigerator to this massive melon! We remove the last watermelon of the year to make room for the Christmas turkey, and the first melon is usually in place before Valentine's Day."

But this wall hanging became something more. Bob subsequently underwent open-heart surgery, and the assemblage of the quilt became a welcome companion for Dixie during her days and nights at the hospital. "Besides the humor that motivated the making of this quilt," she says, "*Fruit of the Bloom* reminds us of our life's ups, downs, gains, losses, and rebirths."

All parts of the watermelon, including the seeds, are appliquéd, with the flowing watermelon vines along the borders done in reverse appliqué.

Susan Webb Lee

Greensboro, North Carolina

Soon after earning degrees in art from two universities, Susan encountered quiltmaking as a way of utilizing fabrics that she had hand-painted. But she soon began to enjoy it for its own sake, and her quiltmaking has resulted in many ribbon-winning wall quilts. Her work has been recognized in national publications and purchased for several private collections around the country.

Susan begins her quiltmaking, as do most quilters, with the selection of fabrics and colors that she feels will work well together. (She almost always includes black.) In the beginning stages of a design, strips, squares, and triangles of fabrics are cut and pinned to a work wall. "I generally have no idea what the final outcome of the quilt will be," says Susan. The fabric shapes are then constantly manipulated—added and subtracted, arranged and rearranged—until a cohesive design emerges. "The most stimulating part of working this way," says Susan, "is the time when all the pieces start to look as though they belong to the same quilt."

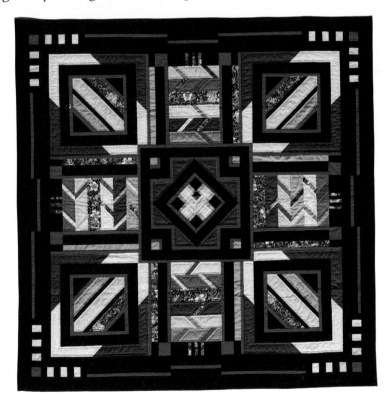

Thunder and Lightning
1985
Thunder and Lightning is fabric expressionism at its best. Just as a thunderstorm demands your attention, so does Susan's dynamic portrayal of the explosion of light and sound, seen and heard in a thunderstorm. Jagged bolts of lightning in narrow fabric strips cut across the background. Flashes of color penetrate the darkness with a knifelike quality. Susan's fabric engineering is so effective, one can almost hear rumbling and crackling.

Michaeline Reed

Pittsburgh, Pennsylvania

Developing ideas, playing with shapes and colors, and figuring out the piecing are Michaeline's favorite areas of quiltmaking. Her inspiration comes from things she observes—children, landscapes, nature, animals, things she reads about, and from her experimentation with shapes and colors. Because of her interest in the design aspect of quiltmaking, the majority of her quilts are original designs.

Her quilts have been exhibited in local shows, banks, and libraries. And one quilt, *Cosmic Wish*, was selected to represent The Fiberarts Guild of Pittsburgh in a traveling show in 1987.

Though a few of her quilts have been sold, Michaeline tells us, "The making of a quilt for me is primarily for pleasure. But when someone purchases one of my quilts, I like knowing that it is being enjoyed."

Enjoy another of Michaeline's wall hangings, *Compass Quest I*, in our "Quilts Across America" chapter.

Flights of Fancy
1987

Michaeline told us she likes to be challenged—the more the better. When a friend returned from a trip to California with an armload of yukata (Japanese fabric), Michaeline leaped at the chance to use this fabulous fabric in a wall hanging. "The challenge was to use the fabric as efficiently as possible in a way that would enhance and not detract from its beauty," says Michaeline. And she accomplished just what she set out to do in *Flights of Fancy*.

The yukata was turned and cut, pieced and folded so that all of it was used, except for a few inches. For a three-dimensional effect, pleats were twisted and accented with ribbon. Printed butterflies and flowers were emphasized with outline quilting. And if you look closely, you'll see an unsuspecting butterfly about to be entrapped by a quilted spiderweb.

A large fabric collection keeps Linda in a constant state of preparedness for quiltmaking. She also maintains records of where she makes her fabric purchases so that she can share with friends and other quilters the history of each fabric that is sewed into her quilts. Leftover drapery fabric was ingeniously employed to make her stunning quilt, *Some Are the Same*, found in our "Starmakers" chapter. And fabrics found in *Persian Paisley*, below, range from a 1950s fabric purchased at an auction to imported English pima cotton to fabric purchased at a garage sale.

Quiltmaking has played a very important role in Linda's life. "When I began to make quilts, it felt very natural and satisfying," says Linda, "as though I had found my niche. I realized that I was combining my lifelong interests of art and sewing."

Linda Goodmon Emery

Derby, Kansas

Persian Paisley
1987

"This quilt is my personal favorite," says Linda. Inspired by the designs of oriental carpets, Linda used over ten different fabrics in the quilt. "Actually," says Linda, "I started with approximately 100 different fabrics but narrowed my selection as my design progressed."

Found in *Persian Paisley* is a bonanza of well-executed quiltmaking techniques: appliqué, reverse appliqué, layered appliqué, and *broderie perse*, to name a few. To outline and accent elements of the design, Linda cut narrow bias strips from an evenly printed fabric and joined the strips to the curved elements of the design. Using bias strips made piecing around the curves easier.

Persian Paisley won First Place and Best of Show ribbons at the 1987 Kansas State Fair in Hutchinson, Kansas, and First Place in the mixed technique (innovative, hand) category at the 18th Annual Quilt Show of the National Quilting Association, Easton, Pennsylvania, in 1987.

RESOURCES

Charlotte Cameron was inspired to make *Summer Stars* after seeing the *Texas Star* quilt in Judy Martin: *Scrap Quilts*. Wheatridge, Colorado: Moon Over the Mountain Publishing Company, pp 33 and 48, 1985.

Dixie Haywood's Japanese crest designs were inspired by those seen in *Traditional Japanese Crest Designs*, edited by C. Hornung. Mineola, New York: Dover Publications, Inc., pp 11 and 44, 1986.

Elizabeth J. Contessa Wuts's *Star-Spangled Banner Scrap Variation* was inspired by the feathered star quilts in Marsha R. McCloskey: *Feathered Star Quilts*. Bothell, Washington: That Patchwork Place, pp 66-68, 1987.

The block pattern for Christine Schnaufer's *Judy's Star Surrounded* is a variation of Marsha McCloskey's Pattern of the Month—*Twisting Star*, ©1985 by Marsha McCloskey. Marsha's pattern was a variation of Judy Martin's Star of the Orient. The Star of the Orient block can be found in Judy Martin: *Scrap Quilts*. Wheatridge, Colorado: Moon Over the Mountain Publishing Company, pp 68-70, 1985.

The block pattern for Donna Lake's *Starry Castle* is a variation of Jinny Beyer's block pattern, Castle Keep. Castle Keep was designed by Jinny Beyer in 1979 and was first published in J. Beyer: *The Quilter's Album of Blocks & Borders*. McLean, Virginia: EPM Publications, Inc., p 109, 1980. It can also be found in J. Beyer: *Medallion Quilts*. McLean, Virginia: EPM Publications, Inc., pp 117 and 141, 1982; J. Beyer: *The Scrap Look*. McLean, Virginia: EPM Publications, Inc., p 36, 1985; and J. Beyer: *Patchwork Portfolio*. McLean, Virginia: EPM Publications, Inc., p 141, 1989.

Donna's scroll quilting pattern is from *Marge Murphy's Heirloom Quilting Designs for Borders and Corners,* ©1980.

Pauline Spieks's *Star and Crescent* was featured in the story, "A Georgia Quiltmaker," found in *Quilt* 7:24, 1985.

For *Compass Quest I*, Michaeline Reed used the oval mariner's compass pattern from C & D Associates, Quilting Notions Mail Order, owned by Crystal Gill, 5521 Sidburn Road, Fairfax, Virginia 22023.

Michaeline's border design is from Jinny Beyer: *The Quilter's Album of Blocks & Borders*. McLean, Virginia: EPM Publications, Inc., p 160, 1980.

Pauline Spieks was inspired to make *Williamsburg Palm* after seeing the *Blue Grove Quilt*, featured in *Better Homes and Gardens Appliqué*. Des Moines, Iowa: Meredith Corporation, pp 76-77, 1978.

Pauline's freezer paper cable border technique was published in A.J. Oliver: "A Cable Border." *Quilt* 6:33, 1984.

The block pattern for Quilt San Diego's *1,001 Nights* can be found in Georgia Bonesteel: *New Ideas for Lap Quilting*. Birmingham, Alabama: Oxmoor House, Inc., p 99, 1987.